Humanics National

INFANT-TODDLER ASSESSMENT HANDBOOK

A User's Guide to the Humanics National Child Assessment Form – Ages 0 to 3

Jane A. Caballero, Ph. D. ● Derek Whordley, Ph. D.

Humanics Limited
P. O. Box 7447
Atlanta, Georgia 30309

Library of Congress Card Catalog Number: 81 - 81660

PRINTED IN THE UNITED STATES OF AMERICA

ISBN: 089 - 334 - 049 - 9

The use of *he* and *she* are not intended to be discriminatory on the basis of sex — rather they are used to vary the language in the text.

Table of Contents

Introduction

Humanics National Infant-Toddler Assessment Handbook is a developmental approach to assessing children from birth-three years of age. Parents and the child development center staff can benefit from the use of this manual. The manual describes how to assess the individual child and how to provide activities that would stimulate the child's development. *Humanics National Infant-Toddler Assessment Handbook* is the user's guide for the Humanics National Child Assessment Form,* a developmental checklist of skills that occur during the first three years of life.

Overview of the Manual

The Humanics National Child Assessment Form (HNCAF), with this accompanying manual, identifies concepts of development through specific behavioral observations. The HNCAF can be easily administered; however, some knowledge of child development concepts should be known if the developmental importance of each item is to be understood.

This manual is presented in two units. The first describes how to assess a child and understand what you are assessing. Since nutrition is a vital part of the development of the young child, an overview of nutrition is also presented.

*THE HUMANICS NATIONAL CHILD ASSESSMENT FORM (Ages 0 - 3) is available from Humanics Limited, P.O. Pox 7447, Atlanta, Georgia, 30309.

The second unit present the Humanics National Child Assessment Form in detail. Each item is presented with the developmental significance of that item and how to observe that behavior. Following are suggested objectives and learning activities for the child who has not mastered the item. The easy-to-make activities can become a vital part of the infant/toddler curriculum.

Who Should Use the Humanics National Child Assessment Form?

The HNCAF with the accompanying manual is designed for parents of young children and the staff of child development programs. The manual is useful for anyone with young children as they plan appropriate learning activities.

This model is especially useful for parent training. The developmental concepts are directly related to the behaviors indicated on the HNCAF. They are easily observed; therefore, concepts of child development can be quickly mastered.

*Humanics National Preschool Assessment Handbook** is designed to assess children from three to six years of age.

---

* HUMANICS NATIONAL PRESCHOOL ASSESSMENT HANDBOOK is available from Humanics Limited, P.O. Box 7447, Atlanta, Georgia, 30309.

UNIT I
PRESCHOOL ASSESSMENT

Chapter I

How to use the Humanics National Child Assessment Form

The Humanics National Child Assessment Form is a checklist of skills and behaviors that a child is likely to develop during the first three years of life. This manual with the accompanying check list is a guide for teachers and parents to use in understanding the importance of providing growth experiences for the young child.

Assessment is a necessary part of the overall teaching process. The Humanics National Child Assessment Form (HNCAF) is designed to help parent and teacher to identify skills and behaviors that the child has developed and to plan learning experiences that facilitate growth. Since children develop at their own individual rates, the checklist is merely a tool for helping identify areas of growth. If the child repeats a certain behavior, you can note these repetitions as indications of developmental progress. The manual and form were designed to help you structure observations so that various levels of the child's growth can be observed. The significance of the behavior and activities to facilitate accomplishment of the behavior follow.

The **HNCAF** is a ninety item checklist of behaviors characteristic of children from birth to three years of age. Broad developmental areas are represented on the four behavior scales of the instrument: **Social—Emotional, Language, Cognitive, Gross and Fine Motor Development.** There are eighteen (18) items under each area.

The items on the scale are presented in a generally progressive developmental sequence. Somewhat easier tasks are followed by more difficult tasks. The form is especially desirable for parental use since they have access to their children over the years. However, the form may be used in any child development setting and is especially valuable if it is used for the three year span.

Chapters Four-Seven present a detailed discussion of each item on the HNCAF. The item to be discussed is first noted, as indicated on the HNCAF. The Developmental Significance, Task Description, Sample Objective and Suggested Activities follow. The Developmental Significance means what is the **importance** of this item. Task Description helps you understand **what behavior to look for** when deciding if the child is able to accomplish the task. The materials or situation you need to provide are specified. When you understand the item, you must decide if the behavior exists for the child. You will record this information on the HNCAF. If the behavior is not present, leave the column blank. If the behavior occurs sometimes, but **not** consistently, put a check in the Appeared column. (You will also need to indicate the date.) You will want to return to these items and do the Suggested Activities with the child.

If the behavior has been mastered and occurs consistently, put a check in the **Occurs Consistently** column. This means the child can perform the task and the Suggested Activities will only be used for reinforcement.

Space has been provided on the HNCAF for assessing the child three times a year. Of course, you can assess the child as many times per year as wished. However, sufficient time between assessments should be allowed so the results can be used in planning and using the **Suggested Activities**. These activities can be used in planning the individual profiles found on the back of the HNCAF. This **Child Development Summary Profile** can provide an overview of the child's progress at a glance. Of course, the Suggested Activities are only that — suggested. You many think of many more. You many want to add your activity at the bottom of the page. We tried to create free and inexpensive items for you to make, but you may have other activities readily available that would help develop the skill.

A sample profile is presented in Chapter Eight to demonstrate the completed use the Humanics National Child Assessment Form.

Who Can Use the HNCAF?

The Humanics National Child Assessment Form was designed for parents and child development staff to use as a simple but useful assessment and planning tool. The items indicated on the form will be easily recognized by adults working with young children. It can be easily administered and the results can be effectively used in planning the learning experiences. Although a center may be responsible for assessing a child and planning adequate experiences, parents are vitally interested in the development of their children. They may not have the time or money to provide a wide variety of store-bought games; therefore, the activities in this manual will be invaluable.

Skills Needed to Conduct the Assessment

Observation skills are necessary in working with young children. These skills can not be taken for granted. They can be taught and enhanced. Training in observation skills can be greatly improved by techniques such as those described by Betty Rowen in *The Children We See.* (Holt, Rinehart and Winston, Inc., 1973). Training exercises such as these will help you to assess the level of development at which the child is operating.

A sample of these observation games follow.

OBSERVATION GAMES

Sensing an Object — Each member of the group is asked to take a small object from his pocket or purse. He is to concentrate on it for a few minutes. Is it smooth or bumpy? Can it make a sound? Does it have any moving parts? How heavy is it? Then he is to put the object away and try to reproduce the sensations he had when he was holding it. When the person has concentrated enough to do this successfully, he may ask others in the group to guess what object he has in mind. (Rowen, p.27)

Changing Appearances — A few people are selected to stand in front of the room while the rest of the group observes everything they can about them. Then they are asked to step outside the room for a few minutes and to make some minor changes in their appearance. The girls might exchange jewelry, while the boys change parts of their clothes. When they return, the group is to determine what changes have been made. (Rowen, p. 27)

Find the Objects — Four or five small objects are placed around the room before the group arrives. They might be a paper clip, a bobby pin, or a rubber band. They are put in places where all can see them, not hidden inside furniture. Students are informed of the four or five objects and told what they are. Time is given for them to be spotted, but not removed from their places. (Rowen, p. 25)

Pantomime of a Daily Activity — Several people at a time are asked to do a pantomime of something they do every day, such as making a bed, brushing teeth, setting a table, and so forth. Others in the group are to focus upon one of the performers to see if his actions are complete and realistic. For example, did he turn off the water and put the toothpaste down when he completed brushing his teeth? (Rowen, p. 27)

Role Reversal — The parties in a two-person situation change places and try to continue the discussion. This is particularly effective in pointing out what it is like to "be in someone else's shoes," as in a parent-teacher conference. (Rowen, p. 20)

The staff and parent must also understand the developmental process. An overview of child development is presented in Chapter 2; however, additional materials should be provided as needed.

Suggested references are found in Appendix A.

The next step is planning for the actual assessment. The following list will be helpful to you in planning the assessment process.

EDUCATION SUPERVISOR'S GUIDE TO PLANNING THE PROGRAM-WIDE DEVELOPMENTAL ASSESSMENT*

1. Determine approximate number of children to be assessed and secure enough copies of the instrument for all new children (if some children are continued for the second year and will have begun an assessment record the prior year, this number will be subtracted from the number of new copies required.)

2. Decide if parents are to be given copies of the assessment form and, if so, secure copies for them.

3. Get copies of the Humanics National Child Assessment Form manual for each teacher or aide, or at least one for each center where the assessment will be administered.

4. Design an assessment training session for staff as described in the text of this manual.

5. Schedule and announce time for assessment observations and timelines for completing the assessments. Make assignments to those responsible for each child's assessment.

6. Inform parents of the assessment and invite their participation (see sample letter in Figure 3). Conduct parent meeting on assessment if possible.

7. Assure that all teachers have the necessary materials to do the assessment (Figure 2) and help them develop lesson plans that include assessment related activities.

8. Conduct assessments and complete the profiles for each child.

9. Schedule time for meetings to develop the Individualized Education Program for each child.

10. Monitor and follow-up to assure that staff understand what to do and that all do it as scheduled.

* Reprinted with permission from Humanics National Preschool Assessment Handbook, Humanics Limited, P.O. Box 7447, Atlanta, Ga. 30309

Few materials are actually needed in the assessment. The following list of materials required for specific items may prove helpful. Additional materials usually found around the home can also be used to create the majority of the suggested activities following each item.

At least three toys or familiar objects should be available for various items.

Item Number	Item
9,61	ball (small and large)
39	food (cracker, raisin)
41	mobile
46	covered package with enclosed items
49	circle, triangle,square & holes of same shape
53	3-4 piece puzzle
59	bottle
71	tricycle
73	rattle
78,79,86,89	eight one inch blocks
83	cup of liquid
84	spoon (some food)
85	book
87	crayon/paper
88	five one inch beads and string
90	buttons

Conducting the HNCAF may take place over a period of time through informal observation, as well as actually participating in an activity with the child. It is up to you to decide when and how it would be conducted most effectively in your particular situation. If discussions among the child's parents, teachers or relatives are possible, then naturally a more reliable assessment would follow.

The results of the assessment will again depend on your particular situation. If you are a parent, then you will want to know what activities to provide your child to enhance his development. If you are in a child development program, then the results can be used to monitor your program's progress and effectiveness. Designing the the program's activities and individualizing the curriculum will also be a benefit derived from this manual. In this case, the first assessment should be as early in the year as possible. Then the second assessment could be given at the end of the year. Since the HNCAF is designed for the first three years of development, it should follow the child during this time span. However, it could be given during the second or even third year of life. If a center initiates the HNCAF, the parents can be encouraged to become involved with the form and Suggested Activities. They will want to know what activities to provide for their children at home. A suggested letter to the parent informing them about the HNCAF follows.

SAMPLE NOTE TO PARENTS INFORMING THEM OF THE PROGRAM'S
INTENTION TO DO DEVELOPMENTAL ASSESSMENT OF THEIR CHILD.

INTENTION TO CONDUCT DEVELOPMENTAL ASSESSMENT

The (name of program) will be conducting a developmental assessment of your child (child's name) along with all other children in our center during the period (date) through (date). This is part of the procedure the center follows in order to plan an individualized educational program for your child.

The Humanics National Child Assessment Form will be used to help structure the observation of your child. This instrument focuses on cognitive development, social-emotional development, gross & fine motor skill development, and the development of language skills. These represent important areas of development for children in the birth to three year age range.

You are invited to join the teacher in conducting the assessment observations of your child. You can receive a copy of the Humanics National Child Assessment Form to complete at home using your own observations. In addition, you can come to the center to do observations of your child engaged in the activities and examine interactions with the other children here. You and the teacher will then be able to compare your observation.

Please contact (teacher's name) at (address) or (phone number) to arrange to receive a copy of the Humanics National Child Assessment From. You can also schedule a time to observe your child at the center.

Sincerely,

_____
Center Director

The Humanics National Child Assessment Form may also be very useful detecting early signs of special problems, such as developmental delays or handicapping conditions. Since this will likely be one of the first screening devices administered to these young children, you may discover a problem that could seriously affect the child's development if undetected.

Special handicapping conditions, especially specific learning disabilities, are often difficult to detect. However, suspected problems can be watched more closely and the child can be referred for a more through examination. Public Law 94-142 has given parents of handicapped children a right, by law, to become involved in program planning and be provided adequate educational opportunities for their children. By law, teachers are also required to notify the parents about special testing they are doing on their child. Therefore, the parent letter (page 16) informing them of the testing will be useful, as well as the IPI form.

Be sure to closly observe the children for behavioral characteristics that may suggest special problems. Watch for the following behaviors:
— Restlessness (hyperactive)
— Easily distracted or lack of interest
— Excessively loud or extremely quiet
— Listlessness, lack of energy
— Limited speech and lack of response
— Poor coordination

TYPES OF HANDICAPPING CONDITIONS

The following list of disability areas and brief indicators that might be observed while administering the Humanics National Child Assessment Form may prove helpful. Remember to seek further help if a problem is suspected.

BLINDNESS or VISUAL IMPAIRMENT: Child constantly avoids close work, is hesitant when moving about the room, is unable to distinguish colors or basic shapes, rubs eyes frequently, trips over things, eyes move in a jerky or uncoordinated manner, frowning or headaches.

DEAFNESS or HEARING IMPAIRED: Child does not respond to sounds, does not socialize or communicate with others, poor or limited speech, must have things repeated, turns ear to speaker, appears inattentive, is excessively loud, balance may be disturbed, frequent earache.

PHYSICAL HANDICAP: Poor coordination, faulty eye-hand movement, fine and gross motor skill poorly developed, stumbles or falls often, unusual body movements or posture, easily tires.

SPEECH HANDICAP: Stutters frequently, substitutes sounds, lisps, strains to speak, irregular speech patterns, pronounces many words unclearly, repeats words often, uses pointing rather than speaking.

HEALTH or DEVELOPMENTAL IMPAIRMENT: History of illness, seizures, easily tires, breathing is difficult, excessively irritable or tense, great or rapid variation in weight.

MENTAL RETARDATION: slow to react, difficulty in understanding and following directions, poor motor coordination, very limited use of imagination, difficulty in paying attention, easily distracted.

SERIOUS EMOTIONAL DISTURBANCE: Cries excessively, has uncontrollable anger, very timid, withdrawn, deliberately inflicts pain or injury on self, uncontrolled shaking or trembling, shows unusual emotional reaction (laughs at sad situation, etc.), inattentive and easily distracted, sits alone for long periods without any entertainment.

SPECIFIC LEARNING DISABILITY: Easily frustrated, short attention span, problems in language development, has trouble distinguishing between similar objects, difficulty in following directions, cannot recognize or identify body parts, poor eye-hand coordination.

Types of Handicapping Conditions reprinted with permission from HUMANICS NATIONAL PRESCHOOL ASSESSMENT HANDBOOK, Humanics Limited, P. O. Box 7447, Atlanta, Ga. 30309.

Chapter 2

Understanding what you are assessing: an overview of child development

Infancy is a stage of vital importance in the life cycle of man where personality development and later learning is first established. Adults, who are caregivers, have a tremendous responsibility to provide nurture and positive experiences for infants in these early months. Infants have a natural curiosity that must be encouraged by the environment if optimum development is to take place. The environment must provide discovery experiences as well as social stimulation by the infants' primary caregivers.

Social interaction is important in the normal development of the child. Skeels, (1966), a noted child developmentalist, matched orphanage children with mentally retarded patients. This experimental group was compared to the *control* group of children who remained in the orphanage setting. The experimental children who had early social contact were well adjusted in later life while the *control* children were maladjusted and not self-supportive. Social relationships are as vital to an infant as material stimulation.

All learning, especially concept development, must be based on actual experiences if it is to meaningful. Adults need to provide tangible experiences for infants. Each new experience is assimilated into the infant's past as he builds up his base of understanding in the world. (Piaget, 1954.)

Research supports the importance of these early years in establishing foundations for later learning. Some theories state that the innate motives and basis for behavior are established during the first three years of life. Hunt's (Havighurst, 1972) extensive work with young children indicated that by restructuring the environment to provide more stimulation, the I.Q. of the child could be raised considerably. Bloom (1964), in his research of human intellectual development, emphasized the importance of the child's early environment by concluding that by the time the child is four years old 50% of his organized thinking patterns are established. It has also been found by Bereiter and Engelman (1966) and others that language structure is formed early in life and is difficult to change. Whether the child is in a home setting, day care center, or family day care home, the primary caregiver must understand that the early environment is crucial for all later development. Consistency of care and nurture are more important than a set curriculum in order to help the baby understand that his world is dependable and secure. Consistency in everyday experiences will build his sense of basic trust.

Such activities as feeding, diapering, and talking can provide opportunities for learning to occur. Gross motor and language development are enhanced during these activities. Stimulation in infancy occurs through the relationship of the infant to his primary caregiver and his interaction with the materials. Every experience of the infant's development, including holding, talking and singing to him will add to his development. His gain depends on his stage of development and past experiences.

Infants begin their development at birth without prior experiences. The baby's natural development can reach maximum potential if caregivers understand developmental phases of growth and provide appropriate stimulation for learning.

DEVELOPMENTAL STAGES

A developmental task is a *task which arises at or about a certain period of the individual's life ——successful achievement of which leads to his happiness and to success with later tasks—— while failure leads to unhappiness in the individuals, disapproval by society, and difficulty with later tasks.* (Havighurst, 1972, pgs. 262-263).

Social reinforcement must accompany the completion of a developmental task for the child to grow up with good feelings about his accomplishment. All babies eventually learn to walk, but the one who receives praise for every step he takes will feel better about himself as well as learn to walk. The baby who has disapproval and constant criticism with each new accomplishment will soon be discouraged with new tasks.

Piaget (1954), a noted Swiss psychologist, has identified developmental stages of growth: *sensorimotor* ((birth-2 years), *preoperational* (2-7 years), *concrete operations* (7-11 years) and *formal operations* (11- up). Infant development falls into this first stage of *sensorimotor* from birth to approximately age two. During that stage babies are aware of sensations rather than external reality. They do not have an awareness of themselves nor do they know where the boundaries of their own bodies end. Learning takes place primarily through the senses. From the neonate stage (first week of life) the baby begins to exhibit some undifferentiated movement. His head is unsteady when held in a sitting position. His hands are usually in a fist; but if he is given an object, he can grasp it and hold it a few seconds before dropping it. The eyes can focus for a short distance and follow the moving light (or object). If the baby's face is stroked, he will turn his face toward that side. A sound such as a rattle or clapping hand will also cause a baby to turn his head in the direction of the stimulus. His main focus of attention is the upper half of the human face. The sucking instinct is strong. Everything goes into the baby's mouth! Hands, nipples, pacifiers help satisfy this sucking need during the sensorimotor stage.

Initially the baby's only communication is crying, but the cries mean different things. He cries during physical discomfort, but also for food, diaper changes or social contact. The caretaker will soon learn to distinguish the meaning of these cries. Soon his sound repertoire will increase to include sounds of satisfaction, gurgles, sighs, babbling, and smiling. At about four weeks, the first consciously-controlled smile will appear. This new awareness of others in his environment indicates his first signs of socialization. When the baby loses his social contact, he will show displeasure.

During the six to nine month period of development the baby can roll himself over in the crib. He can at first sit steadily with support and then by himself. He gains interest in his body parts. His feet, as well as his hands, go into the mouth. He learns a wide range of motor skills from rocking on his hands and knees to clapping his hands. Gradually he develops use of thumb and finger in opposition. Then he will want to use much manipulative exploration such as grasping a rattle and shaking it with a jerky motion or pulling a string for an out-of-reach toy. He will show a negative reaction to strangers and object to separation from his mother. This *stranger anxiety* concept indicates his growing awareness of others. His language repertoire gradually includes gestures to convey meanings and responses to tones of voices and familiar words such as *bye-bye, mommy, daddy,* or his own name.

During the nine to twelve month period the baby becomes mobile, crawling and maybe walking. Stairs can add to his challenge of crawling, but he may crawl up and then be unable to crawl down. Now he has reached the stage Piaget refers to as *object permanence*. This means that the baby can retrieve an object if placed out of sight. Prior to the stage of object permanence, an out of sight object would be out of mind — it does not exist for him.

This is a time for much manipulative exploration, such as placing one cube on top of another, placing blocks in a cup, clapping his hands, throwing, and picking up objects. These oppositional movement tasks (use of thumb and fingers) provide problem solving activities. Mastery of these skills enables him to feed himself. Gradually he begins to imitate others in his environment doing such things as combing hair, putting lids on pots, and studying himself in the mirror. He now waves bye-bye, responds to simple commands such as No, and uses a few simple words.

By the time the baby is twelve to eighteen months old, he begins walking and using his arms for balance. He still crawls for fast locomotion. He can bend over to pick up an object, throw objects, and respond to rhythm. Though he does not understand the conceptual meaning of language, he utilizes expressive jargon. He can show his desires, respond to picture books, and follow directions. By eighteen months, he can imitate a horizontal crayon stroke and put blocks in a cup.

The period of child development from eighteen to thirty-six months encompasses the sensory motor period described by Piaget and the preconceptual period. There are vast differences between the accomplishments of children as they progress from the end of one level and into the higher reaches of the other. Physical movement, language development and social behaviors readily reflect these developments.

At the younger end of the scale, motor development continues to improve but at a slower rate than in earlier months. This has some consequences in terms of continuing to explore environments. There is some degree of caution and relative lack of skill in moving around. The three year old, by contrast, seems positively agile, jumping, galloping and running around at will.

In terms of social behaviors and play phenomena, it is apparent that three year olds are anxious to please parents and teachers, have some sense of following directions, can stay on task for a minute or two, relate to other children and seem to enjoy their world. This is in stark contrast to children half their age. In the eighteen months preceeding this three year old level, young children advance from egocentric activity to the trials and tribulations of parallel play and the ultimate sacrifice of sharing and relating to others. They move from mistrust of unknown persons, overcome the panic of mother leaving the room for a minute and move into the unknown territory of relating to other children and adults.

Marked differences in language occur throughout this period. The development of increasing language competency differentiates both the play and social transactions in which children become involved. The business of naming items supplants the more basic issue of object permanence. It then flourishes to include phrases and fragments of utterance and advances into full blown statements, unending questions, and constant attempts to redescribe the world through the mysteries of semantics and syntax.

Notions of time, numbers, shapes and sizes are all intriguing new dimensions in the life of three year olds. They mean little a mere year and a half earlier. Their humor, imagination, developing self concepts and pride in themselves successfully emerge from those basic foundations dealing with the sounds of language, building of memory, and experiments with movement which are such crucial issues only months before.

REFERENCES

Bereiter, C. and S. Engelman. *Teaching Disadvantaged Children in the Preschool.* Englewood Cliffs, N.J.: Prentice-Hall, 1966.

Bloom, Benjamin S. *Stability and Change in Human Characteristics.* New York: John Wiley and Sons, Inc., 1964.

Erikson, Erik. *Childhood and Society.* New York: W.W. Norton & Company, Inc., 1951.

Havighurst, Robert J. *Developmental Tasks and Education,* Third Edition. New York: D. McKay, Co., 1972.

Hunt, J. McV. *Intelligence and Experience.* New York: The Ronal Press Co., 1961.

Piaget, Jean. *The Construction of Reality in the Child.* New York: Basic Books, Inc., 1954.

Skeels, H.M. *Adult Status of Children with Contrasting Early Life Experiences.* Monographs of the Society for Research in Child Development, Serial No. 105, Vol. XXXI, No. 3, 1966.

Chapter 3
Nutrition

The importance of nutrition in the development of the young child should not be minimized. The young child's ability to learn is greatly affected by nutrition in the early years of life. It is an established fact that the brain is the fastest growing organ in the human from the time of birth. The first two years of life are critical for brain growth. Even prenatally, the brain is affected by nutrition. Poor nutrition in infancy and early childhood can cause irreversible brain damage. Severe malnutrition is not prevalent in the United States; however, even moderate undernutrition can cause children to lag behind in their studies. Children who come to school hungry may be disruptive and inattentive. They may not even want to try to learn.

Dietary habits are formed early in life. Children are not born with definite likes and dislikes for certain foods. A positive attitude toward nutritious foods must be established early. Children are prone to eat "junk food". They often eat in a hurry, not experiencing well-prepared foods. Mealtime should also be a time to talk and share with the family. We, as teachers and parents, need to be aware of the importance of proper nutrition in the development of the child. Showing the relationships between nutrition and growth with parents and colleagues is of utmost importance.

Many of us know very little about feeding an infant. How many of the following questions can you answer correctly?

Circle the correct answer.

1. Is a fat baby a healthy baby?
     yes   no

2. During the first year of life the baby's weight normally
     doubles   triples   quadruples

3. If you limit the bottle feeding, will the baby be encouraged to eat more solids?
   yes   no

4. Does cow milk have the sufficient amount of vitimins and minerals for a human baby?
   yes   no

5. Is it all right to save one formula from feeding to feeding?
   yes   no

6. Should baby food or milk be taken directly from the refrigerator and given to the baby?
   yes   no

7. Is it necessary to burp the baby after feeding?
   yes   no

8. Is the baby hungry every time he cries?
   yes   no

9. If your baby does not like water, should you stop giving it to him?
   yes   no

10. Is propping a bottle with a pillow a good way to feed the baby?
   yes   no

Answers

1.	no	6.	no
2.	triples	7.	yes
3.	yes	8.	no
4.	no	9.	no
5.	no	10.	no

If you didn't score 100% you will want to pay special attention to the next section. We will try to provide some ideas on how to add to the nutritional development of your child.

BABY'S FOOD

Baby food does not **have** to be bought in little jars! We will provide a few suggestions on how to prepare your own food, basic nutritional requirements, and how to plan your baby's diet.

Cooking

Baby food can be cooked in a variety of ways to conserve nutrient value. **Steaming** is an easy and excellent way to preserve nutrients. Most stores have inexpensive steams (under $5) that can be placed in a variety of different sized pots. Heavy gage wire can even be molded to fit a pot. The vegetable can then be placed above one inch of boiling water. Be sure the pot has a tight fitting lid. It only takes a few minutes to steam the vegetables.

Boiling is acceptable; however, use as little water as possible. If the cooking water is used in other cooking, such as to liquify purees, the nutrients will be eaten. Foods can also be **roasted** or **broiled,** but you may need to use other fluids (such as the boiling water above.)

MEATS

Because an infant grows rapidly, he needs more and more food at adjusted schedules. Start by feeding a new meat by putting a small amount on the tip of a spoon. Add more each day and use the same meat for 3—4 days, so he can get used to this new food. Introduce one meat at a time.

One serving of baby meats should be prepared as follows. Put 1/2 cup cooked meat, cut into small pieces, and 3 tablespoons of milk, formula, or liquid from the meat into a blender. (Be sure to remove the fat and waste from the meat.) Blend the meat until the desired consistency is achieved. Store it in a clean, sterilized container. Meat should be strained. Beef, liver, veal, lamb and chicken are all good choices.

The canned baby meats are easy to use if you don't prepare your own. Be sure to dispose of meat left in a meat jar.

EGGS

Egg yolk puree can be prepared by boiling an egg for 15-20 minutes. Remove the shell and yolk. Puree with one tablespoon of formula or milk.

VEGETABLES

Vegetables should be fed to the baby in the same way as the meats. Start by putting a small amount on the tip of the spoon. Add more each day and use the same vegetable for 3-4 days. Soon he'll eat 2-4 tablespoons of a vegetable at a time.

Carrots, squash, peas, green beans, beets, and spinach are all good to serve. Cut or tear cooked or canned vegetable into chunks and put into a blender with 2 table-spoons of formula, milk, or liquid from the vegetable. Blend them to the desired consistency and store them in a clean container.

FRUITS

Fruits should be fed to the baby in the same way as meats and vegetables. You can use strained baby fruit in jars or canned fruit. Canned peaches, pears, or apples can be mashed through a strainer and fed to the baby. Very ripe bananas can be mashed and fed raw. One-half of the canned or cooked fruit can be placed in a blender with 2 teaspoons of liquid from the fruit and blended to desired consistency. Three-fourths cup of raw fruits can be placed in a blender with 1 teaspoon fruit juice or 1 teaspoon lemon juice (to prevent darkening) and blended to desired consistency.

Fruit juices can be prepared in the blender by simply liquifying the fruit. If the drink is too thick, thin with water, fruit juice, or formula.

Your infant's feeding schedule should be supervised by your pediatrician. The following helpful hints are only presented as an idea for what you'll be feeding an infant.

Birth — 3 weeks		Milk, formula
3 weeks	8-10 am	Cereals (rice, barley, oatmeal)
	4-5 pm	Add formula to thin-gradually thicken. Feed by spoon. Give boiled water between bottles.
6 weeks	8-10 am	Cereal (l-2 T. and formula)
	4-5 pm	
	1-2 pm	Introduce new fruits (such as banana)
2 months	8-10 am	Cereal (1-2 T. and formula), apple (cherry) juice
	1-2 pm	Introduce new vegetables with 1-2 T. fruit
	4-5 pm	Cereal, fruit, vegetable, formula
3 months	7-10 am	Cereal (3-4 T. and formula), apple juice
	1-2 pm	Introduce new meat with vegetable, fruit, cereal
	5-6 pm	Gradually add new meat (instead of cereal), vegetable, fruit
4 months		Continue pattern, increase portions
5 months	8-10 am	Cereal, fruit or juice, formula. Add orange juice and hard cooked egg yolk.
	1-2 pm	Meat and vegetable (l/2 to l jar), pudding and dessert (l/2 jar), formula
	5-6 pm	Meat, vegetable, fruit, formula
6 months	8-10 am	Egg yolk and wheat cereal. Crackers, toast can be given to baby to chew on (first step in self feeding). Fruit juice between meals (2-4 oz.)
7 months		Table foods-mashed (lightly seasoned)

SPECIAL NOTE:
Your child may be following a completely different schedule. The trend is to delay solid foods until four (4) months of age.

Learning activities utilizing food can be integrated into various curriculum areas related to motor skill development, communications, science, and social interactions. Various educational and commercial sources have developed learning activities which can be used in making nutrition education an exciting component of the early childhood program. The following bibliography suggests current resources.

Asmussen, P.D.: SIMPLIFIED RECIPES FOR DAY CARE CENTERS. Cahners Books, 221 Columbus Ave., Boston, MA 02116, 1973, 217 pp., $12.95.

Assoc. for Childhood Education International: COOKING AND EATING WITH CHILDREN-A WAY TO LEARN. ACEI, 3615 Wisconsin Ave., N.W., Washington, D.C. 20016, 1974, 48 pp., $2.50.

Ault, R. and L. Uraneck: KIDS ARE NATURAL COOKS. Houghton Mifflin Co., One Beacon Street, Boston, MA. 02107, 1974, 129 pp., $6.95.

Cadwallader, S.: COOKING ADVENTURES FOR KIDS. The San Francisco Book Co., Houghton Mifflin Co., 2 Park Street, Boston, MA., 02107, 1974, 101 pp., $6.95.

Cohl, V.: SCIENCE EXPERIMENTS YOU CAN EAT. J. B. Lippincott Co., Philadelphia, PA., 1973.

Cooper, J.: LOVE AT FIRST BITE. Alfred A. Knopf, New York, 1977, $3.50.

Croft, K.B.: THE GOOD FOR ME COOKBOOK. Order from Karen B. Croft, 741 Maplewood Place, Alto, CA. 94303.

Ferreira, N.J.: THE MOTHER CHILD COOKBOOK — AN INTRODUCTION TO EDUCATION. Pacific Coast Publishers, 4085 Campbell Ave., Menlo Park, CA. 94025, 1969, 73 pp., $2.95.

Florida Dept. of Education: EXPLORING FOODS WITH YOUNG CHILDREN — A RECIPE FOR NUTRITION EDUCATION. Food and Nutrition Management Section, Florida Department of Education, Tallahassee, FL. 32304; 1977, single copy free.

Goodwin, M.T. and G. Pollen: CREATIVE FOOD EXPERIENCES FOR CHILDREN. Center for Science in the Public Interest, 1755 S. Street, N.W., Washington, D.C.,20009, 1974, 191 pp., $4.50.

Hatfield, A.K. and P.S. Stanton: HELP! MY CHILD WON'T EAT RIGHT. Acropolis Books LTD, 2400 17th St., N.W., Washington, D.C. 20009, 1973.

McClenahan, P. and I. Jaqua: COOL COOKING FOR KIDS. Fearon Publishers, Inc., 6 Davis Dr., Belmont, CA. 94220, 1976, 170 pp., $6.50.

Paul, A.: KIDS COOKING WITHOUT A STOVE: A COOKBOOK FOR YOUNG CHILDREN. Doubleday and Co., Inc.,Garden City, New York, 1975, $5.95.

Ratner, M. and T.T. Cooper: MANY HANDS COOKING. Catalog No. 5032, UNICEF, 331 East 38th St., New York, 10016, 1974, $4.00.

U.S.D.A.; FUN WITH GOOD FOODS. Stock No. 001-000-03868-1, Superintendent of Documents, U.S. Government Printing Office, Washington, D.C. 20402, 1978.

UNIT 2
THE HUMANICS NATIONAL CHILD ASSESSMENT FORM

Chapter 4

Humanics National Child Assessment Form: Social-Emotional Development

SOCIAL-EMOTIONAL DEVELOPMENT

The emotional development of the child deals with his self-concept development and the ability to express and control his feelings. Social development refers to his ability to get along with others.

The self-concept is the image a person has of himself. Early in life the parent transmits negative or positive feelings toward the child. Eye contact, body contact, expressions, and tone of voice all influence the child's feelings of worth. Being positive with the child will encourage him to develop a positive self-concept. A child needs attention and will often seek it at inconvenient times. Speaking in a positive manner to the child is important, even if you don't have the time to be with him. The interaction a child has with you establishes his self-concept. A positive self-concept enables a person to use his abilities more freely. An inadequate self-concept limits what the person can do. The development of the child's self-concept is essential to his happiness and chances for future success.

A child who feels good about himself will develop self-discipline and self-control. He will learn to develop his abilities and wait for the attention he deserves. Learning to express feelings in an acceptable fashion is a necessary part of growing up. The infant will cry when hungry or wet. Later he will learn to express his feelings in a more mature fashion. For example, if he is hungry, he'll say, "I'm hungry. I need something to eat," instead of crying for someone to try to satisfy this need. Being able to express feelings in a positive manner is a very difficult thing for one to do. A child who has been discouraged from displaying emotions or expressing himself may have a difficult time later in life when relating to other people.

This book is designed to get you involved. Some items only have one activity described. Try to think of other activities and write them in spaces provided at the bottom of the page.

Focuses on Face

Focuses attention on face of another person.

DEVELOPMENTAL SIGNIFICANCE:

The baby needs to have various experiences in order to respond to visual stimulations. His awareness of the face is one of the first focal points of interest, and he needs to have loving caretakers available to him to focus his attentions on. His self-concept is greatly enhanced through this awareness.

TASK DESCRIPTION:

Encourage the child to play in front of a mirror.

SAMPLE OBJECTIVE:

To recognize himself in a mirror.
To begin to identify body parts.

SUGGESTED ACTIVITIES:

1. Place the child in front of a mirror. If she is put on a sink in the bathroom, stay with her. Do not leave the child unattended on a high surface. If she is placed in front of a tall mirror, be sure it is well secured so it will not fall over.

2. Hold her in front of the mirror. Point to her and call her by name. Say: "There you are. I see ————."

3. Point to body parts. Point to them in the mirror. Help the baby touch his reflection.

Responds to Voice

Turns head in response to voice.

DEVELOPMENTAL SIGNIFICANCE:

This will give the child practice in hearing the spoken language and prepare her for responding to language.

TASK DESCRIPTION:

Talk to the baby.

SAMPLE OBJECTIVE:

To develop auditory awareness.

SUGGESTED ACTIVITIES:

1. Talk to the child at every opportunity. Talk to her when you change her diaper, feed her, bathe her or just for the fun of it.

2. Put her in a safe place near you when you are doing your chores. Explain what you are doing. "Mommy is putting the clothes away."

3. Describe everything to her. Help her get used to hearing you speak.

3 Smiles Responsively

Returns smile after seeing another person smiling.

DEVELOPMENTAL SIGNIFICANCE:

The child's self-concept is greatly enhanced when he responds to a person's smile. It demonstrates to the child that a smile represents positive reinforcement.

TASK DESCRIPTION:

Give the child a toy, speak to him and smile.

SAMPLE OBJECTIVE:

To elicit a smile from the child.

SUGGESTED ACTIVITIES:

1. Provide the child with a favorite toy. Talk and smile as you play with the toy. Pass the toy back and forth, smiling as you receive it.

2. Write your own activity.

 Discriminates Wants

Pushes away something not wanted.

DEVELOPMENTAL SIGNIFICANCE:

This will help the child begin to distinguish between what he likes and what he dislikes.

TASK DESCRIPTION:

Present the child with some object or foods that are known to be disliked.

SAMPLE OBJECTIVE:

To encourage initial decision-making.

SUGGESTED ACTIVITIES:

1. Present the child toys, foods, or objects which are known to be unattractive to him. Allow him time to respond.

   NOTE: The intent is not to reinforce "dislikes" but to help the child to discriminate between items which are "liked" and "disliked".

2. Write your own activity.

3 Plays independently (I)

Plays alone for short periods of time.

DEVELOPMENTAL SIGNIFICANCE:

The child is encouraged to become independent of the caretaker. This represents a change in the bonding relationship between mother and child which existed at birth.

TASK DESCRIPTION:

Provide the child with appropriate toys (mobile, rattle, doll, stuffed animal) and leave his presence.

SAMPLE OBJECTIVE:

To give the child an opportunity to engage in egocentric play.

SUGGESTED ACTIVITIES:

1. Select a preferred, safe, durable toy for the child to manipulate in a crib, playpen, or other secure place. Initiate a playful and pleasing activity and gradually leave his presence. Extend the period of absence from a few seconds to a few minutes.

2. Write your own activity.

 **Plays Peek-a-boo**

Plays peek-a-boo or smiles when you appear in peek-a-boo games.

DEVELOPMENTAL SIGNIFICANCE:

This represents *object permanence*. Objects remain in existence even though they are out of sight. The child only begins to realize this concept when he is about nine months old.

TASK DESCRIPTION:

Play peek-a-boo games with the child, hiding yourself and other objects from the child's sight.

SAMPLE OBJECTIVE:

To help the child develop the concept of object permanence.

SUGGESTED ACTIVITIES:

1. Hide your face under a blanket while sitting in front of the child. As you remove the blanket, smile and say "Peek-a-boo!"

2. Put the child's toy, such as a doll or car, under a blanket or box, while he is watching. Encourage the child to remove the item that is covering his toy to retrieve the object.

Presents objects

Hands object such as a toy to another person.

DEVELOPMENTAL SIGNIFICANCE:

The child learns to release toys and objects to someone else and feels secure in doing so. Be sure to keep the toys in sight of the child to reassure him that they do not disappear.

TASK DESCRIPTION:

The child learns to exchange one preferred toy for another.

SAMPLE OBJECTIVE:

To initiate exchange. This is a prerequisite to sharing.

SUGGESTED ACTIVITIES:

1. Give the child a toy which he likes. Then present him with a favorite toy, which he will prefer to exchange for the first. He will hand one to you in exchange for the second. The number of exchanges can grow by the introduction of other toys which the child likes. This will also encourage gross motor development.

2. Write your own activity.

 Plays Simple Game

Plays simple rhythm games such as pat a cake with others.

DEVELOPMENTAL SIGNIFICANCE:

This will build a relationship between rhythmical and rhyming patterns of language and motor activity. The coordination of eye-hand movements is initiated.

TASK DESCRIPTION:

Play rhythm games with the child to help him follow directions with hand movement using an oral stimulus.

SAMPLE OBJECTIVE:

To show relationship between patterns of sounds and patterns of movement.

SUGGESTED ACTIVITIES:

1. Sit the child in front of you and repeat the rhythm as he watches your facial expressions and body movements.

    Pat-a-Cake

    Pat-a-cake, pat-a-cake, baker's man
    Bake me a cake as fast as you can.
    Pat it, and pat it and mark it with a "B"
    Bake it in the oven for (name) and me.

2. Write your own activity.

40

 **Plays Catch**

Plays "catch" with another person by rolling a ball back and forth.

DEVELOPMENTAL SIGNIFICANCE:

The child is moving towards a new level of interaction with a significant adult in which an object is continuously exchanged. This is different from earlier learnings in which one object is exchanged for another.

TASK DESCRIPTION:

Play with the child while sharing an object.

SAMPLE OBJECTIVE:

To encourage play between two people.

SUGGESTED ACTIVITIES:

1. Wad up a piece of newspaper and secure it with masking tape. Children can use this ball without fear of being hit by a harder ball. The size can also be easily varied. (A hoop can also be made by rolling the newspaper and then attaching the ends together with masking tape.)

   Variation: Fill a sock with newspaper and ball it up.

2. Sit on the floor with legs apart. Roll or gently bounce the ball between persons.

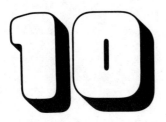 Makes Wants Known

Points or calls to get desired object.

DEVELOPMENTAL SIGNIFICANCE:

The child uses verbal and/or non-verbal signals to indicate preferences between a group of objects or for a particular item.

TASK DESCRIPTION:

The child will be encouraged to use language and/or non-verbal communication in making choices.

SAMPLE OBJECTIVE:

To help the child choose one or more desired objects.

SUGGESTED ACTIVITIES:

1. Present the child with a selection of three to four foods and/or three or four toys. Ask him, "Which one do you want?" After he receives it, repeat the question. Continue the activity until the child has received the objects he desires.

2. Write your own activity.

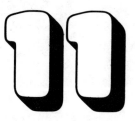 **Shows Familiar Object**

Offers or shows a toy to another child.

DEVELOPMENTAL SIGNIFICANCE:

This represents a level of social development which is more advanced than the earlier types of "exchanges". During this period the child is able to take toys or other objects with which he has built associations and to offer them, or at least show them, to another person.

TASK DESCRIPTION:

Provide opportunities for the child to relinquish a toy to another, or at least show it off to someone else.

SAMPLE OBJECTIVE:

To encourage sharing of toys with which the child has significant associations.

SUGGESTED ACTIVITY:

Allow the child to play with a safe familiar object. A simple safe object that can be made is a stocking doll. Cut the top off the stocking. Cut it in half lengthwise to form two tubes. Stitch the arms. Cut partway through lengthwise for legs. Stuff it with filling. Stitch and attach the arms. The neck can be formed by tying a ribbon and a face can be embroidered. Dress it with an old sock or other material.

 Plays Independently (II)

Plays independently of other children, occasionally interacting with them.

DEVELOPMENTAL SIGNIFICANCE:

The emergence of parallel play is an important step in the child's socialization process. His totally egocentric behavior gives way to sharing.

TASK DESCRIPTION:

Provide two or more children with appropriate toys and leave their presence.

SAMPLE OBJECTIVE:

To give the child an opportunity to engage in parallel play.

SUGGESTED ACTIVITIES:

1. Select safe and durable toys for the children to manipulate. Leave their immediate presence so they will feel free to play independently. (Item 5). They will begin to play with other children.

2. Write your own activity.

Talks to Other Children

Talks or babbles to other children while playing near them.

DEVELOPMENTAL SIGNIFICANCE:

As parallel play between children is developed they have increasing needs to communicate with each other verbally. The interjection of language into play situations enhances the socialization process. Needs, wants, and thoughts may be expressed.

TASK DESCRIPTION:

Encourage opportunities that promote social interaction through language.

SAMPLE OBJECTIVE:

To provide an environment in which initial communication skills can be developed.

SUGGESTED ACTIVITIES:

1. As in Item 12, provide a space in which a number of toys are available for two children to play with. If language is prompted by the first selection of objects, provide new materials to arouse curiosity and interchange.

2. Write your own activity.

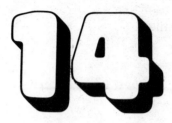

Begins Removing Clothing

Removes at least one piece of clothing, such as a sock.

DEVELOPMENTAL SIGNIFICANCE:

While removing clothing is a psychomotor activity, it can be used as part of the socialization process in which the child helps an adult to accomplish a task. This helping behavior, in which language should be encouraged, represents a further step in the building of relationships.

TASK DESCRIPTION:

Combine language and action in a "helping situation."

SAMPLE OBJECTIVE:

The child assists the primary caretaker while being undressed, and opportunities are taken to build new vocabulary or reinforce known words during the encounter.

SUGGESTED ACTIVITIES:

1. At bedtime ask the child to pull off a sock or similar article of clothing. Use expressions such as:
   a. "Can you help me by . . ."
   b. "Thank you for being my helper . . ."
   c. "It's great to have someone to help me . . ."
   d. "You are such a good helper . . ."

2. Elaborate on the helping theme in other situations, e.g., cleaning up time following snacks and when putting toys away after a play activity.

 **Identifies Familiar Person**

Refers to a familiar person by name.

DEVELOPMENTAL SIGNIFICANCE:

The child has recognized the association between a person and his name.

TASK DESCRIPTION:

Provide experiences for the child to identify familiar people.

SAMPLE OBJECTIVE:

To identify a known person in the child's environment.

SUGGESTED ACTIVITIES:

1. Show family photographs to the child. Point to various family members and ask who they are.

2. As a later activity, ask the child to identify significant objects which belong to members of the family, e.g., "Daddy's hat," "Susie's doll," or "Mike's bike."

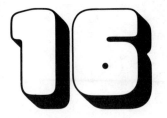

Knows Own Name

Says first name when asked for it.

DEVELOPMENTAL SIGNIFICANCE:

The child's self-concept is built as he learns more about himself. He must first realize he is a unique person with his own particular name.

TASK DESCRIPTION:

Encourage self-identification experiences.

SAMPLE OBJECTIVE:

To make the child aware of and respond to his own name.

SUGGESTED ACTIVITIES:

1. Take a picture of the child. Glue it to a piece of construction paper. Write his name under the picture. Point to the picture and say the child's name.

2. Substitute the child's name in rhyming games.

One day (child's name) and Mommy fell out
And what do you think it was all about?
Mommy liked coffee and (child's name) liked tea
That was the reason they could not agree.

Interacts With Other Children

Chooses to join a group of 2-3 children
for a short time.

DEVELOPMENTAL SIGNIFICANCE:

This will illustrate that personal behavior is modified by interaction when several others are present. Self-control is needed and relationships need to be established.

TASK DESCRIPTION:

Provide environments in which children have good possibilities for a variety of social interactions.

SAMPLE OBJECTIVE:

To provide opportunities for children to want to interact with others.

SUGGESTED ACTIVITIES:

1. Give each child a musical instrument (pots, pans, spoons, empty oatmeal boxes, etc.) Play marching music on the record player. March in a circle and comment on the activity. "Lara is beating her drum."

2. Dance with the baby as you hold him in your arms.

3. During snack time, have the children sit around a table and encourage them to pass and share food and drink.

4. Play rhythm games.

> *Ring-around-the-rosie.*
> *Pocket full of posies,*
> *Ashes, ashes,*
> *All fall down.*

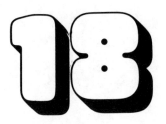

Expresses Feelings

Uses words to express feelings of happiness, sadness, and anger.

DEVELOPMENTAL SIGNIFICANCE:

To learn to express oneself in an acceptable fashion is a vital skill necessary to emotional well-being. Children need to understand that it is normal and acceptable to have a variety of feelings.

TASK DESCRIPTION:

Provide the child with opportunities to talk about feelings.

SAMPLE OBJECTIVE:

To learn to openly express a variety of emotions.

SUGGESTED ACTIVITIES:

1. Present the child with a variety of pictures showing people in various emotional situations, e.g., a small boy opening up a present. "How do you think he feels today?" Show a picture of a little girl who just fell off her tricycle and is crying. Ask the child, "How do you think this little girl feels?"

2. Present various textures to the child and ask him how they make him feel. Ask him, "How do you feel when you touch this?" (See picture.) Cut an outline of the child's hand and apply a texture (burlap, sandpaper, tin foil, etc.) to each finger.

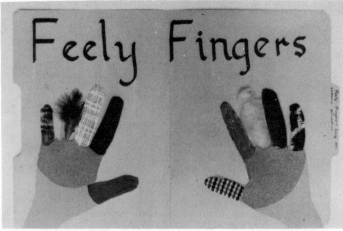

Chapter 5

Humanics National Child Assessment Form: Language Development

LANGUAGE DEVELOPMENT

Language development can be divided into two parts — receptive language and expressive language. Receptive language refers to the language the child takes in. This language intake forms the basis of thought. Of course it precedes expressive language. The emergence of expressive language occurs about eighteen months and continues throughout life. However, by the time the child is four, his language acquisition is highly developed. The young child understands more than he can say. He must have the opportunity to hear and imitate language. Language helps him express himself and learn to develop his concept of self.

Language begins at birth. The infant must hear sounds so he can imitate them. By four-five months, the child has mastered the babble stage and begins to imitate the sounds he hears. By the time he is one year old, he can make meaningful sounds, such as ma-ma and da-da. By the time the child is two, he will have added words that represent objects and actions, such as "Me want" (points) or "Go by-by." He later begins to put words together into phrases. By age four, he should be able to speak in longer utterances that are similar to sentences.

According to Madorah Smith,* the child's vocabulary consists of:

Age 3   896 words
Age 4   1540 words
Age 5   2072 words
Age 6   2562 words

The Templin Study** provides a sequence in the child's ability to pronounce consonant sounds:

Age 3   m,n,ng,p,f,h,w
Age 3.5   y
Age 4   k,b,d,q,r
Age 4.5   s,sh,ch
Age 6   t,th,v,l
Age 7   z,zh,j

* Smith, Madorah E "An Investigation of the Development of the Sentence and the Extent of Vocabulary in Young Children." (University of Iowa Studies Child Welfare, 3:5, 1926).

**Templin, Mildred C. "Certain Language Skills in Children," Institute Child Welfare Monograph Series XXVI. (Minneapolis: University of Minnesota Press, 1957) p. 174.

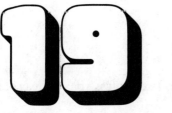

Laughs

Laughs out loud.

DEVELOPMENTAL SIGNIFICANCE:

This represents a beginning awareness that vocalization can create an emotional response. Being able to laugh out loud is a pleasurable behavior to the child. The infant will respond to the pitch of the voice and touch of the body and laugh out loud.

TASK DESCRIPTION:

Position the baby on his back and hold the baby's arms out. The parent or teacher says, "I'm going to kiss you." Then he/she will nuzzle and kiss the bellybutton, fingers, or toes.

SAMPLE OBJECTIVE:

To stimulate the child to make a pleasurable response to some external stimulus.

SUGGESTED ACTIVITIES:

1. Walk your fingers from the baby's toes to the baby's neck. Make a noise as you run run your fingers over the baby's body.

2. Hold a toy over the baby's face. Move the toy back and forth in front of the baby's face.

SPECIAL NOTE: See end of chapter for various language development activities.

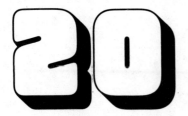

Utters Speech Sounds (I)

Makes two different speech sounds, (examples: ba, da, ca, etc.).

DEVELOPMENTAL SIGNIFICANCE:

This represents a beginning stage in copying sounds. The child imitates a sound made by parent/teacher and is given positive reinforcement. He's beginning to understand that his sounds have an effect on the person listening to him.

TASK DESCRIPTION:

This gives the child an opportunity to copy beginning sounds after hearing a variety of language sounds.

SAMPLE OBJECTIVE:

To encourage imitation of sounds.

SUGGESTED ACTIVITIES:

1. Get down on the floor with the baby. Have the baby on his back and place his hands on your face. Softly say two sounds "Ma Da". After you say the sounds take his hands away and wait for a response. Hug, kiss and smile when he responds.

2. Call the child by his full name. Make up songs to sing to the baby. Talk to the baby as though you know he is listening and understanding.

Babbles Responsively

Babbles back in response to adult talking.

DEVELOPMENTAL SIGNIFICANCE:

This gives an early indication of auditory development and an ability to make sounds in response to adult language patterns.

TASK DESCRIPTION:

This allows the child to hear and to repeat a number of sounds.

SAMPLE OBJECTIVE:

To encourage a response to adult language.

SUGGESTED ACTIVITIES:

1. Call the child by his full name. Show the child a colorful mobile or wall picture. Point out various objects or colors in the picture/mobile. Wait for a response and continue to talk to the child. Repeat the sounds you hear.

2. Hold the baby in a sitting position (on changing table) and bend so that you are on eye level with him. Talk softly to him and tell him what you are going to do. "We are going to change your diaper now and then we're going outside. Want to go outside?" Repeat the question until he babbles a response and then praise him.

 Connects Sounds

Strings different sounds together without meaning.

DEVELOPMENTAL SIGNIFICANCE:

This represents a beginning awareness that vocalization and playfulness go together. He is beginning to understand that his sounds express his needs or feelings.

TASK DESCRIPTION:

This provides opportunities for the child to respond to an activity verbally.

SAMPLE OBJECTIVE:

To encourage the child to respond verbally.

SUGGESTED ACTIVITIES:

1. Sit the baby in the high chair and show him a squeeze toy. Squeeze it until it makes a sound and then hide it behind your back. Wait for the child to make sounds until you repeat the activity.

2. Place the baby in front of a mirror. Make sure the baby notices himself in the mirror. Listen for sounds. Talk to the child about his reflection, if necessary.

3. Be physical with the baby. Sit on the floor. Bring your knees to your chest. Lean the baby on your shins so that baby's head extends over the knees. Lay back so that your head touches the floor. Keep your legs stiff and let the baby "ride" on your legs. Raise to the original position. Repeat this as long as it is fun. Repeat the sounds you hear to the baby.

 Repeats Same Sound

Says dada or mama (or equivalent) without specific reference to parent (s).

DEVELOPMENTAL SIGNIFICANCE:

This represents a patterning of beginning sounds, which can later be tied to a point of reference.

TASK DESCRIPTION:

This provides the baby with opportunities to find a pleasurable sound and associate it with a pleasurable activity.

SAMPLE OBJECTIVE:

The child should begin to establish a reference point for speech.

SUGGESTED ACTIVITIES:

1. Hold baby on your lap facing you. Take his hands and let him stroke your face while saying mama or dada. Encourage him gently to repeat the sounds. Then take his hands in yours and stroke his face and say mama or dada.

2. After a period of quietness, play the piano or sing to your baby. Encourage the child to join in, using pots, pans, and spoons.

3. Baby will often babble the same sound while playing alone. Acknowledge your baby's response.

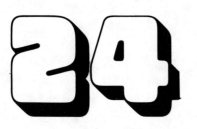 Utters Speech Sounds (II)

Makes four different speech sounds.

DEVELOPMENTAL SIGNIFICANCE:

This represents a beginning form of labeling based on visual discrimination and the sense of touch.

TASK DESCRIPTION:

This encourages the child to make speech sounds.

SAMPLE OBJECTIVE:

This may help the child to develop specific sounds.

SUGGESTED ACTIVITIES:

1. Cover four empty toilet paper rolls with different fabrics. Hand each one to him and wait for him to make a sound. Repeat until he utters one different sound for each roll.

2. Read sound books to the child, encouraging him to say the sounds after you.

Imitates Sounds

Imitates sounds others make.

DEVELOPMENTAL SIGNIFICANCE:

This represents a continuation of the child's vocabulary development. She is beginning to associate certain sounds or words with objects.

TASK DESCRIPTION:

This provides an experience for the child to learn sounds from others.

SAMPLE OBJECTIVE:

This may encourage the child to associate sounds with objects.

SUGGESTED ACTIVITIES:

1. Sit on the floor across from baby. Roll a ball to the baby and have her roll it back. Tell her to say, "ball". When she says it, roll it back to her and praise her.

2. Act out the song: **This is the Way**

> *This is the way we wash our face,*
> *Wash our face, wash our face.*
> *This is the way we wash our face.*
> *So early in the morning.*
>
> (Other verses:
> . . .brush our teeth
> . . .brush our hair
> . . .eat our breakfast
> . . .take a bath)

Refers to Parent (s)

Says dada or mama (or equivalent) in reference to parents.

DEVELOPMENTAL SIGNIFICANCE:

This represents labeling. The child understands that the parent has a name and will respond favorably when called by his/her name.

TASK DESCRIPTION:

This helps the child to respond correctly in identifying her caretakers.

SAMPLE OBJECTIVE:

This should direct the child to a significant caretaker.

SUGGESTED ACTIVITIES:

1. Sit the baby in her high chair. Sit in a chair in front of her and put a blanket over your face. Tell her to say mama/dada. When she says it, take the blanket off and say mama/dada.

2. Show the child a picture of each parent. Say the appropriate word as you point to each parent's picture. Praise the child for correctly identifying each parent.

3. Each time your child says mama or dada (without reference to you as a parent), make a response, e.g., "Yes, I'm your mama."

Responds to Instructions

Responds to simple instructions such as no, come here, stop.

DEVELOPMENTAL SIGNIFICANCE:

This represents an initial introduction to following directions. The child is beginning to understand that certain words relate to boundaries or limits of his actions.

TASK DESCRIPTION:

This allows opportunities for the child to begin to respond to the instructions of another person in a manner that demonstrates understanding.

SAMPLE OBJECTIVE:

This may help the child to relate words to specific actions.

SUGGESTED ACTIVITIES:

1. Put the baby in her high chair and sit in front of her. Hold a spoon in your hand and bang on the tray. Say "stop" and stop banging. Give the baby the spoon and have her bang. Then say "stop". Then bang and stop together.

2. Within the home, indicate boundaries and limits. Change the tone of your voice and say "stop" whenever the child steps out of bounds.

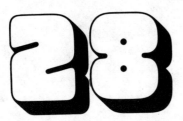

Identifies picture

Points to appropriate picture when told "Show me the ————."

DEVELOPMENTAL SIGNIFICANCE:

The child shows a broadening of her knowledge. The child demonstrates her ability to associate particular images with words.

TASK DESCRIPTION:

This helps the child understand that words can be labels for objects. He is beginning to learn how to use his functional beginning vocabulary.

SAMPLE OBJECTIVE:

This helps the child associate words with pictures.

SUGGESTED ACTIVITIES:

1. Have a picture of a single object. Name the object. Ask the child to name the object.

2. Paste pictures of animals (or any category) on cardboard cards. Show the pictures to your child calling each animal by name. After some time, the child should be able to associate each picture with a word.

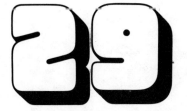

Verbally Identifies Need

Uses words to make wants known.

DEVELOPMENTAL SIGNIFICANCE:

It is important that the child speaks when he wants to make a statement or express a feeling. If the parent/teacher interprets for him, then he is learning that gesturing or crying will elicit a response. He should be encouraged to make his needs known through speaking.

TASK DESCRIPTION:

The child knows his needs and can communicate those needs in a manner that is understandable by the caretaker.

SAMPLE OBJECTIVE:

This should help the child express needs through words.

SUGGESTED ACTIVITIES:

1. When the baby wakes up from a nap, talk softly to him and hold your arms out. Ask him what he wants. "Do you want to get up?" Wait until he says it before you do it. Ask him if he's hungry. "Do you want some milk?" Wait for him to say it before you offer it.

2. Write your own activity.

 Speaks Words

Has ten definite words in vocabulary.

DEVELOPMENTAL SIGNIFICANCE:

He's learning that objects have a label and is also learning that in order to identify objects, he must use the correct label.

TASK DESCRIPTION:

The child is encouraged to express words that he already knows.

SAMPLE OBJECTIVE:

The child is extending the beginning process of labeling objects.

SUGGESTED ACTIVITIES:

1. Put ten different familiar objects in a bag. Ask the child to reach in, pull out the object and identify it.

2. Show the child his toys. Identify each item to the child. After identification, ask the child what each item is. When the child correctly speaks the word, praise him.

3. The caretaker turns on the cassette tape player while the child speaks. Listen to find the words that he says.

Makes Own Sentences

Makes three-word sentences (Not just repeating parents' words).

DEVELOPMENTAL SIGNIFICANCE:

The child is beginning to show a comprehension of the syntax of language. Patterns of words have more impact than labels.

TASK DESCRIPTION:

This provides the child with an opportunity to put together words to form a sentence.

SAMPLE OBJECTIVE:

The child should be able to make a response in sentence form that expresses his thoughts.

SUGGESTED ACTIVITIES:

1. Select a three or four step routine that the child has. The routine might be getting dressed, bath time, etc. Identify each step of the routine to the child. After a period of time, while following the routine, ask the child what happens next. Wait for a response. Change the routine and look for a response.

2. Write your own activity.

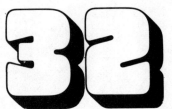

Indentifies Position

Can show the location of an object; that is under, behind, or in front of.

DEVELOPMENTAL SIGNIFICANCE:

The child is beginning to learn concepts that denote depth perception. The child is aware of spatial differences and is beginning to understand that these differences can be named.

TASK DESCRIPTION:

This provides actual experiences for the child to learn location.

SAMPLE OBJECTIVE:

He should learn new concepts of space which show the location of an object; that is under, behind, or in front of.

SUGGESTED ACTIVITIES:

1. Select one concept to teach to the child; e.g., under, over, behind, in front of. All week point out situations or create examples to show meaning to the concept. For example, **under:** Place the child's shoes under the bed, eggs under the toast, silverware under the napkin, toys under the bed or chair, money under the book. Ask, "Where are the shoes? Where is the silverware?"

2. Find a large cardboard box and cut two openings in it large enough for your baby to crawl through. He will learn spatial concepts as well as coordination of large muscles. Reinforce the concepts and words: through, around, in, out and under.

3. Put three small cars under, behind, and in front of three boxes. Tell the child to give you the car that is under, behind and in front of each box.

4. Read and point to the position of the characters in *Little Miss Muffet*.

Little Miss Muffet
Sat on a Tuffet,
Eating her curds and whey.
Along came a spider,
And sat down beside her,
And frightened Miss Muffet away.

 **Answers Questions**

Answers simple questions, who and what.

DEVELOPMENTAL SIGNIFICANCE:

This represents another level of response in giving answers.
The child's responses are made specific as to who and what.

TASK DESCRIPTION:

This provides the child with opportunities to communicate.

SAMPLE OBJECTIVE:

The child should be able to answer simple questions, who and what.

SUGGESTED ACTIVITIES:

1. Have some objects hidden in a box or in a pot with a lid. Open the box and hold the object and ask him what it is. The objects should be familiar, such as a ball, spoon, fork, etc.

2. Place two items before the child. Tell the child to cover his eyes. Remove one of the items. Ask the child to name the missing item. Increase the number of items as appropriate.

3. Show a photograph of familiar family members and ask, "Who is this?"

Forms Plurals

Adds 's' to words to form plurals.
(example: dogs, books)

DEVELOPMENTAL SIGNIFICANCE:

The child is learning that in order to communicate the idea of more than one object he needs to change words. The beginning concept of more and less is also being introduced. This is an additional refinement in language use. He is learning informally and unconsciously.

TASK DESCRIPTION:

Interact with the child to refine language.

SAMPLE OBJECTIVE:

To learn through informal and unconscious activity a new rule of language.

SUGGESTED ACTIVITIES:

1. Play a game with the child in which he fills in the appropriate word. For example, one boy, two —–—. Play this game in the car in order to take advantage of the visual stimuli.

2. Place a book in front of the child and ask him to tell you what it is. Then place five more books in front of him and ask "What are these?"

3. Make the puppets of the three pigs and a wolf. Ask the child to identify one, two and three pigs. End the activity by reading and acting out the story of "The Three Little Pigs."

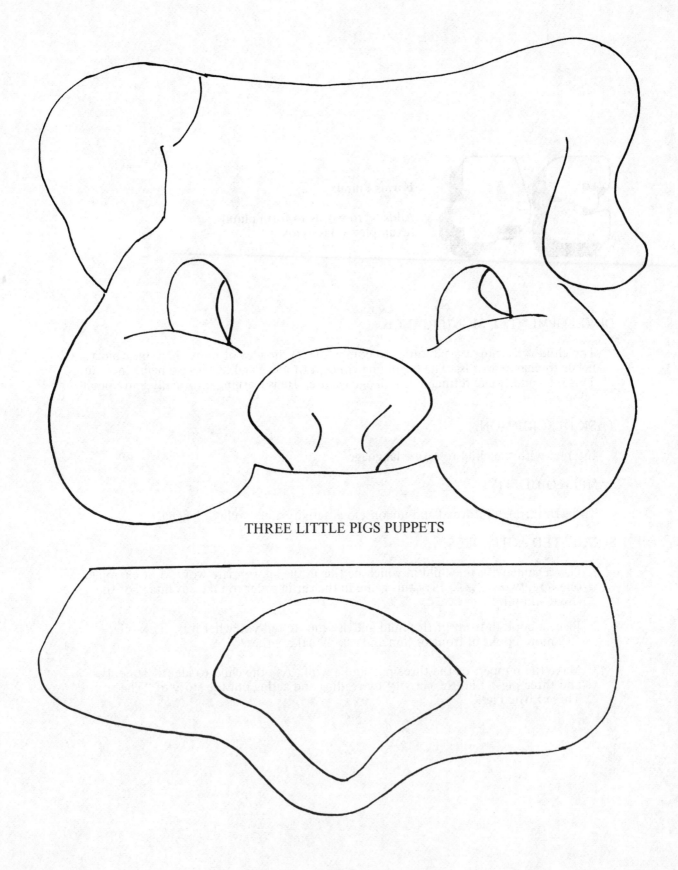

THREE LITTLE PIGS PUPPETS

WOLF PUPPET

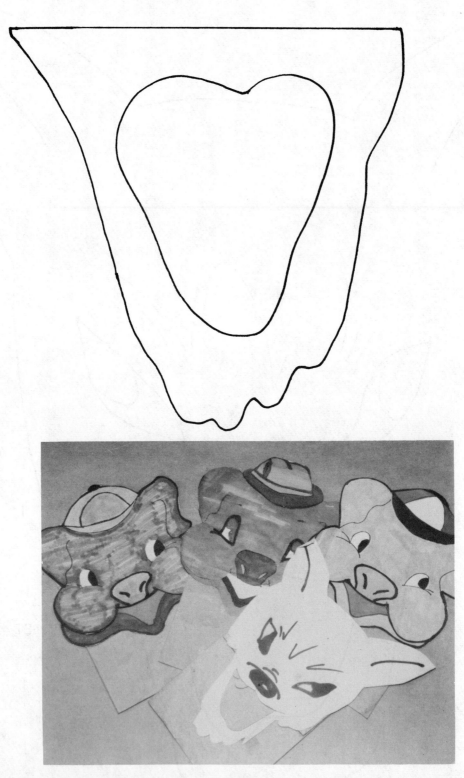

Color and attach head to top flap of paper bag. Attach mouth pieces to paper sack half way under the top flap. The characters will "talk" as you move your hand. Make three pigs and one wolf.

Identifies Action

Identifies action in pictures.
(example: "The dog is running.")

DEVELOPMENTAL SIGNIFICANCE:

The child is learning that different actions have a name. Actions that he can do also have a name.

TASK DESCRIPTION:

Use illustrations to associate words and action.

SAMPLE OBJECTIVE:

To help the child learn to associate words with actions.

SUGGESTED ACTIVITIES:

1. Show the child different action pictures of children. For example, a baby crying, a girl sleeping, a boy playing. Ask him what the people are doing.

2. Ask the child to move in certain ways. For example, show me how you hop, show me how you run, show me how you walk.

3. Show pictures of children doing certain movements or activities and ask the child if he can imitate the movement. For example, "Can you hop like an Indian?"

 **Combines Thoughts**

Can express two thoughts combined. (For example "When mommy comes, I'm going home.")

DEVELOPMENTAL SIGNIFICANCE:

The child's thought processes are expanding. The child is beginning to be more complex in his sentence structure.

TASK DESCRIPTION:

This provides an environment for the child to increase the amount of oral language.

SAMPLE OBJECTIVE:

This should permit the child to express a sequence of ideas.

SUGGESTED ACTIVITIES:

1. Ask the child to do two things. Let the child ask the adult to do two things. Increase the number of activities.

2. Carefully select pictures of other children at work or play. Show the picture to the child. Ask what the child is thinking or to tell you what is happening. Engage in a discussion about the picture. Begin by letting the child fill in part of the story. The was a little girl named————. Increase the length of the sentence and the number of blanks.

CRITERIA FOR SELECTING BOOKS FOR INFANTS AND TODDLERS

1. The illustrations in books should be simple and bright. They should reflect experiences with which the child is familiar or have sufficient associations to which the child can relate.

2. The story content should be within the comprehension of the child. Short, well written prose passages are generally more acceptable than extended pieces of writing.

3. Where illustrations are excellent, but the language used by an author is difficult, be prepared to devise new language to tell the child about the pictures.

4. Use the story lines to reinforce earlier learnings and to create associations with new concepts and ideas.

5. Avoid printed material which may confuse, frighten or frustrate the child.

6. Identify books which coincide with family experiences and show a range of situations known to the child. Domestic events, new births, marriages, divorces, deaths, travel experiences and social relationships are examples. The experience of reading these materials should be positive and helpful.

7. Recognize that books come in all sorts of shapes, sizes, and colors. Choose a variety and encourage the child to handle them with care.

8. Maintaining attention and interest are crucial. Short pieces full of excitement, humor, and a range of experiences known to the child are important.

TEACHING LANGUAGE AT MEALTIME

Teaching language at mealtime can also be an excellent learning situation. Toddlers are very interested in their food and this provides an easy subject for conversation.

1. Praise children who are eating with their utensils, sitting still, and drinking without spilling.

2. Don't nag children to eat.

3. Respond to the child when he asks questions or asks for seconds.

4. Encourage the child who is not eating to try new foods.

5. Ask questions about food such as: "What color is the food? What kind of food is it? Where does it come from? What does it taste like?"

6. When the child is finished eating, you may ask questions such as: "What did you eat most today? What did you like least?"

POEMS, FINGERPLAYS AND SONGS FOR INFANTS AND TODDLERS

Did You Ever See a Lassie

Did you ever see a lassie, a lassie, a lassie,
Did you ever see a lassie do this way and that?
Do this way and that way and this way and that way,
Did you ever see a lassie do this way and that?

(Move as you say the verse: Jump, hop, clap, sit, etc.)

Hokey Pokey

Put your ––––in, put your ––––out,
Put your ––––in and shake it all about.
Let's do the hokey pokey,
And we turn ourselves about.
That's what it's all about.

(Substitue various body parts in the blanks, e.g.
right hand, whole body, left leg.)

London Bridge

London Bridge is falling down,
Falling down, falling down.
London Bridge is falling down,
My fair lady!

Mulberry Bush

Here we go round the mulberry bush,
The mulberry bush, the mulberry bush.
Here we go round the mulberry bush,
So early in the morning.

This is the way we clap our hands,
Clap our hands, clap our hands.
This is the way we clap our hands,
So early in the morning.

(Substitute various actions, e.g., stamp our
feet, sweep the floor.)

Old MacDonald

Old MacDonald had a farm, E I E I O
And on this farm he had a (animal name), E I E I O.
With a (animal sound) here, and a (animal sound) there,
Here a (animal sound), there a (animal sound), everywhere a (animal sound)
Old MacDonald had a farm, E I E I O.

Where is Thumbkin?

Where is thumbkin? Where is thumbkin? (Hide extended thumbs behind back)
Here I am! Here I am! (Bring thumbs out)
How are you today sir? Very well, I thank you! (Wiggle thumbs)
Run away! Run away! (Hide thumbs again)

(Other verses:
pointer, tall man, ring man, pinky)

Baby Bumble Bee

I'm bringing home a baby bumblebee,
Won't my mommy be so proud of me! (Hold imaginary bee in hands)
I'm bringing home a baby bumble bee,
Bzzzzzzzz
Ouch! The bee stung me! (Separate hands quickly)

I'm a Little Teapot

I'm a little teapot short and stout,
Here is my handle, here is my spout.
(Hand on hip, other hand extended)
When I get all steamed up,
Hear me shout:
Tip me over and pour me out.
(Lean over)

Eency-Weency Spider

The eency-weency spider went up the water spout
(Thumb and index finger creep up)
Down came the rain and washed the spider out.
(Bring hands down and out)
Out came the sun and dried up all the rain.
(Make sun with hands over head)
And the eency-weency spider went up the spout again.

Two Little Blackbirds

Two little blackbirds, sitting on a hill.
(Hold up forefingers)
One named Jack and the other named Jill.
Fly away Jack, fly away Jill.
(Hide each finger behind back)
Come back Jack, come back Jill.

Row Your Boat

Row, row, row your boat
Gently down the stream
Merrily, merrily, merrily, merrily
Life is but a dream.

The Bus Song

The people on the bus go up and down
Up and down, up and down.
The people on the bus go up and down,
All through the town.
(Other verses:
. . .horn goes beep, beep, beep
. . .driver says "Move on back"
. . .baby goes "Waah, waah, waah!"
. . .mother says "Sh, sh, sh")

Other favorite nursury rhymns are:

Old King Cole
Jack Sprat
Little Boy Blue
Little Jack Horner
This Little Pig
Jack Be Nimble
Hickory, Dickory, Dock
Baa, Baa, Black Sheep
Humpty Dumpty
Jack and Jill
Rub a Dub Dub
The Old Woman Who Lived in a Shoe
Bye, Baby Bunting
Hey, Diddle, Diddle
Mary Had a Little Lamb

Ten Little Indians

One little, two little, three little Indians,
Four little, five little, six little Indians,
Seven little, eight little, nine little Indians,
Ten little Indian boys.

Create 2 blackbirds for the poem *Two Little Blackbirds.*

Folded Paper Puppet

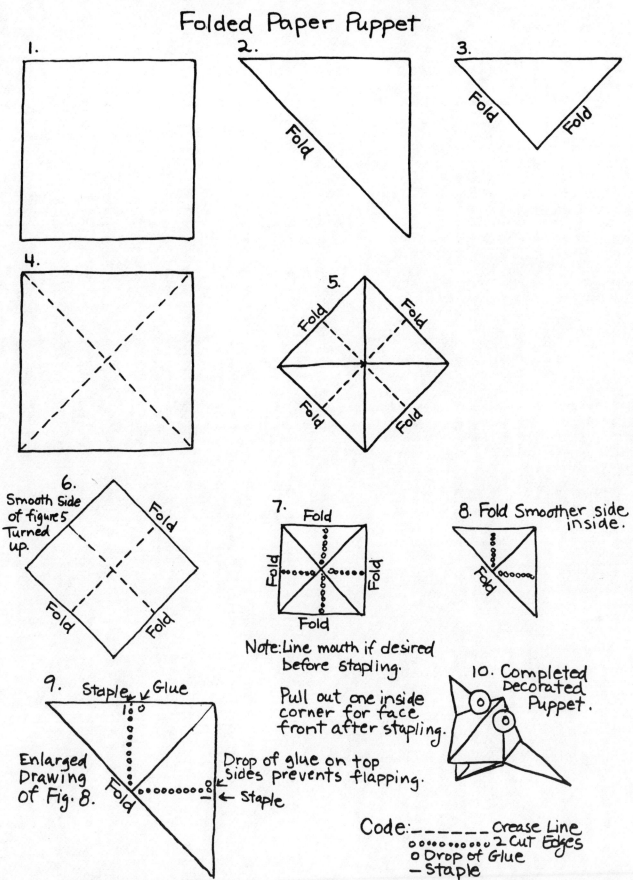

1.

2. Fold

3. Fold Fold

4.

5. Fold Fold Fold Fold

6. Smooth Side of figure 5 Turned Up. Fold Fold Fold

7. Fold Fold Fold Fold

8. Fold Smoother side inside. Fold

Note: Line mouth if desired before stapling.

Pull out one inside corner for face front after stapling.

9. Staple Glue

Enlarged Drawing of Fig. 8. Fold

Drop of glue on top sides prevents flapping.

← Staple

10. Completed Decorated Puppet.

Code: _ _ _ _ _ Crease Line
o o o o o o o 2 Cut Edges
o Drop of Glue
— Staple

Chapter 6

Humanics National Child Assessment Form: Cognitive Development

COGNITIVE DEVELOPMENT

Cognitive development refers to the thinking patterns of the child. The process begins at birth and continues until the child reaches intellectual maturity. Jean Piaget, the noted Swiss psychologist, has greatly influenced our understanding about the intellectual growth. He has identified four stages of cognitive growth: *sensorimotor, preoperational, concrete operations,* and *formal operations.* Although the chronological age may vary, the progression remains the same.

In the first stage, *sensorimotor,* the child learns through the senses and manipulation. The approximate age range is from birth to two years. He must organize his sensory-perceptions into an internal "Schema" (structure) and coordinate various images. He becomes aware that objects remain the same when viewed from different angles. Constancy is the characteristic phrase.

The second stage, *preoperational,* relates to the child from approximately two-seven years of age. Objects begin to represent something. Gestures, words, and pictures begin to have symbolic meaning. The child classifies things by a single feature (such as size). He is not concerned about contradictions between size and weight such as when a large light object floats and a small heavy object sinks. The characteristic phrase is irreversability. As the child emerges into the intuitive phase of the preoperational stage, he gradually becomes aware of mass, weight, and volume.

The *concrete operations* stage (approximately seven-eleven years of age) is the third stage. The child begins to think out problems previously worked out with concrete objects. Logical thought emerges.

The last stage, *formal operations,* is from the approximate age range eleven–fifteen. The child can deal with abstraction only after he has passed through the previous stages.

The importance of recognizing the first two stages is vital in assessing the infant and toddler. Sensory-concrete experiences are necessary if the child is to progress to logical mature thinking. He must have the opportunity to explore and manipulate objects in his environment. Associations can only be made if he has this stimulating free environment to explore. As the child's cognitive processes develop, memory grows. Recognition of parents or familiar objects occurs during infancy, but may not last long. When an object or person is removed from the environment, the object no longer exists. Piaget refers to this as object permanence. As the child grows, his memory will increase until more complex thoughts emerge.

Imagination is another aspect of cognitive growth. Imagination refers to the ability to take acquired knowledge and use it in a new situation. Encouraging the child to use imagination will help him realize there is not always one right answer. This obviously will help him adjust to the "real" world.

Solving problems is a more complex aspect of cognitive development. The infant may grab a dangling mobile, thus solving a problem. As he grows, his problems become more complex and he must be allowed to solve them. Adults often try to do everything for their child, preventing him from having this necessary growth experience. We should try to provide the child with problem-solving activities and allow him to solve them.

Explores Object

Carries object in hand to mouth.

DEVELOPMENTAL SIGNIFICANCE:

The child explores his world through tactile and taste experiences. His senses are a primary means for the exploration of his world.

TASK DESCRIPTION:

Allow the child to play with safe exploratory objects.

SAMPLE OBJECTIVE:

To explore objects using taste and touch.

SUGGESTED ACTIVITIES:

1. Place a number of safe objects in front of the child. Encourage him to pick them up. In most instances anticipate an intuitive response— the child will put the object in his mouth.

2. Write your own activity.

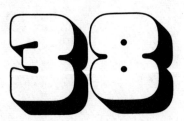 Connects Sight with Sound

Looks in Direction of Sound.

DEVELOPMENTAL SIGNIFICANCE:

This will help the child develop eye coordination, body-eye coordination and eye-hand coordination.

TASK DESCRIPTION:

Play sound games with the child to encourage aspects of body coordination.

SAMPLE OBJECTIVE:

To teach the child to identify sounds.
To track a noise-making object.

SUGGESTED ACTIVITIES:

1. Get the child's attention by shaking the keys in front of him. Slowly raise the keys in front of him while continuing to shake them. Encourage him to raise his head and chest.

2. Place the baby in a lying position on his back. Stand near him but out of his line of vision. You will want him to watch a noise-making object such as a rattle, sound cans or set of keys rather than you. Shake the object in front of the child's face until you get his attention. Then bring it from baby's side to the center of his head. Repeat. Notice how he follows the object with his eyes Repeat, holding the object on the opposite side of his body.

3. Sounds cans can be made out of film cans or similar containers. Put the same objects into two different cans. The child can shake the cans. Later he can match the two cans that sound alike as an auditory activity.

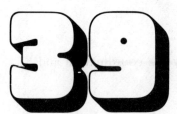

Discriminates Need

Accepts only milk or food; rejects other objects if placed in mouth when hungry.

DEVELOPMENTAL SIGNIFICANCE:

The child must learn to satisfy his needs. Hunger, the most basic need, must be satisfied. The child's sucking impulse will eventually give way to actually sucking a bottle or eating foods as he learns to respond to this need.

TASK DESCRIPTION:

Provide experiences that will encourage the child to eat food, not other objects, when he is hungry.

SAMPLE OBJECTIVE:

To encourage the child to respond to his hunger needs.

SUGGESTED ACTIVITIES:

1. Present the child with food that he likes, such as a cookie or juice, and other safe items, such as a small toy or block. Encourage the child to place the food, NOT the toys, in his mouth.

2. Write your own activity.

40

Follows Falling Object

Looks for an object after seeing it fall.

DEVELOPMENTAL SIGNIFICANCE:

This will refine visual development with particular reference to eye focus.

TASK DESCRIPTION:

Stand or kneel in front of the child and drop an object from below and above eye level.

SAMPLE OBJECTIVE:

To encourage the child to watch an object as it drops.

SUGGESTED ACTIVITIES:

1. Get the child's attention by telling him you are going to drop a ball. Stand in front of him and drop the ball from various heights.

2. Write your own activity.

Sustains Activity

Pulls repeatedly a cord attached to overhead bells or mobile.

DEVELOPMENTAL SIGNIFICANCE:

This represents an early stage of eye-hand coordination based on visual discrimination. The child is visually aware of an object and is able to use his hand to cause the mobile to move.

TASK DESCRIPTION:

Attach a mobile within reach of the child on his bed.

SAMPLE OBJECTIVE:

To promote eye-hand coordination.

SUGGESTED ACTIVITY:

Tape the top of a coat hanger with wool or material and wind it around the hanger until it is covered. Hang four or five pieces of string from the hanger. Draw children (faces or other objects) on tagboard. Cut out and attach to the string. Hang the mobile over the crib.

Red hair
White skin

Black hair
Brown skin

Blond hair
White skin

89

Black hair
Brown Skin

Brown hair
White skin

Black hair
Yellow skin

Black hair
Brown skin

Blonde hair
White skin

Black hair
Yellow skin

Brown hair
White skin

Finds Partially Hidden Toy

Finds and exposes partially hidden toy.

DEVELOPMENTAL SIGNIFICANCE:

The baby needs to become aware that objects continue to exist even though they are out of sight. Piaget refers to this emerging concept as "Object permanence."

TASK DESCRIPTION:

The caretaker is encouraged to play "hide and seek" with objects.

SAMPLE OBJECTIVE:

To establish object permanence in the mind of the child.

SUGGESTED ACTIVITY:

Cover a box with colorful contact paper. Put safe items into the box—items that can not be swallowed such as clothes pins, jar lids, measuring spoons, and bells. Place the box a short distance from the baby or put the box on its side so some of the objects can be seen. The baby can move the box to see the unexposed items and take the objects out of the box.

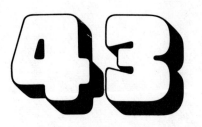

Retrieves Objects

Pulls strings to obtain object attached to it.

DEVELOPMENTAL SIGNIFICANCE:

This is an initial stage of body control. Being able to obtain an object that is desired and within sight indicates that the child has achieved a certain amount of eye-hand coordination.

TASK DESCRIPTION:

To allow the child to reach out and pull a string in order to obtain an object.

SAMPLE OBJECTIVE:

To help the child grow in his ability to pull objects—gross motor development.

SUGGESTED ACTIVITY:

Fasten a cord through one end of a box and knot the cord on each side of the hole. Cover the box with colorful contact paper. Put the box within reach of the child. He will want to retrieve it. Interesting objects may be placed in the box to make it more desirable to retrieve it. The sounds made by the objects in the box will attract the child.

Locates Desired Object

Moves object aside in order to reach another desired object.

DEVELOPMENTAL SIGNIFICANCE:

This task indicates that the child realizes that an obstruction to an object may be removed in order to reach the item that is needed.

TASK DESCRIPTION:

The child is able to locate a desired object by moving another object.

SAMPLE OBJECTIVE:

To manipulate his environment to obtain things that he wants.

SUGGESTED ACTIVITIES:

1. Have the child place a row of blocks on a table. Place another row in front of the first row. Encourage the child to remove the first row in order to reach the second row of blocks.

2. Take a favorite toy, such as a doll or car, and cover it with a blanket. Encourage the child to remove the blanket to retrieve the toy.

 Searches For Hidden Object (I)

When hidden object is moved from one place to another, child continues to search in first place.

DEVELOPMENTAL SIGNIFICANCE:

This is a second stage in reinforcing the concept of object permanence. (Refer to Item 42).

TASK DESCRIPTION:

The child will find an object that is hidden within a larger container.

SAMPLE OBJECTIVE:

To learn that things continue to exist when out of sight.

SUGGESTED ACTIVITIES:

1. Assemble materials: shoe box, larger box, paper sack, toys small enough to fit into the box, but too large to swallow. Show the baby a toy and place it in the box and close the top. Shake the box and say, "Can you hear that noise?" "See if you can find the toy." To make the game harder, hide the toy in the box and then hide the box in a sack. Help the baby open the box, if he has too much trouble.

2. Write your own activity.

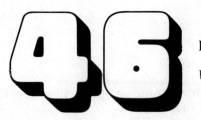

Reveals Hidden Objects

Unwraps a covered package to discover its contents.

DEVELOPMENTAL SIGNIFICANCE:

The child will be encouraged to think about objects which are covered and take action to retrieve them.

TASK DESCRIPTION:

Encourage the child to unwrap a covered package.

SAMPLE OBJECTIVE:

To be able to unwrap a package. This supports motor skill development.

SUGGESTED ACTIVITIES:

1. Put a few safe items (sponge shapes, measuring spoons, small doll, bells, etc.) in a medium sized box. Cover the box with colorful wrapping paper. Give the box to the child and allow him to open it.

2. Write your own activity.

 Searches for Hidden Object (II)

When hidden object is moved from one place to another, child searches in the new place.

DEVELOPMENTAL SIGNIFICANCE:

This is yet another stage in building object permanence.

TASK DESCRIPTION:

Interact with the child by playing with a "Feely Bag."

SAMPLE OBJECTIVE:

To encourage the child to retrieve hidden objects.

SUGGESTED ACTIVITIES:

1. Make a small bag or sack out of colorful material with a draw string at the top. Identify selected interesting items. Place them as shown in the picture. Talk to the child about objects being outside of the sack and inside of the sack. Play with the items outside the sack, then put them inside and recover them.

2. For a more advanced task, encourage the child to identify the objects in the bag without looking at them. Identification of objects by touch will increase sensory awareness.

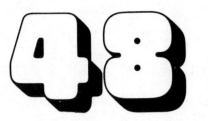 **Identifies Body Parts**

Points to three parts of own body.

DEVELOPMENTAL SIGNIFICANCE:

The child begins to label objects in his environment with special reference to his own body.

TASK DESCRIPTION:

The child will identify parts of his body by naming and touching them. He will then transfer these learnings to more abstract experiences with stuffed and cardboard body parts.

SAMPLE OBJECTIVE:

To identify the arms, legs, and feet.

SUGGESTED ACTIVITIES:

1. Cut out two shapes of a hand, leg or feet in sturdy material. Sew around the edges leaving a small opening to stuff the shape with cotton. Complete the stitching.

2. Cut out shapes of body parts from a complete outline of a human figure. Ask the child to place them together in an appropriate way.

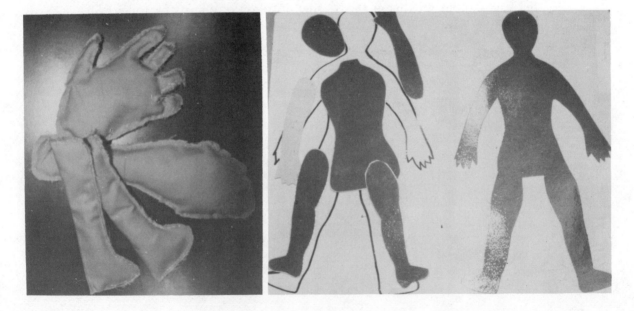

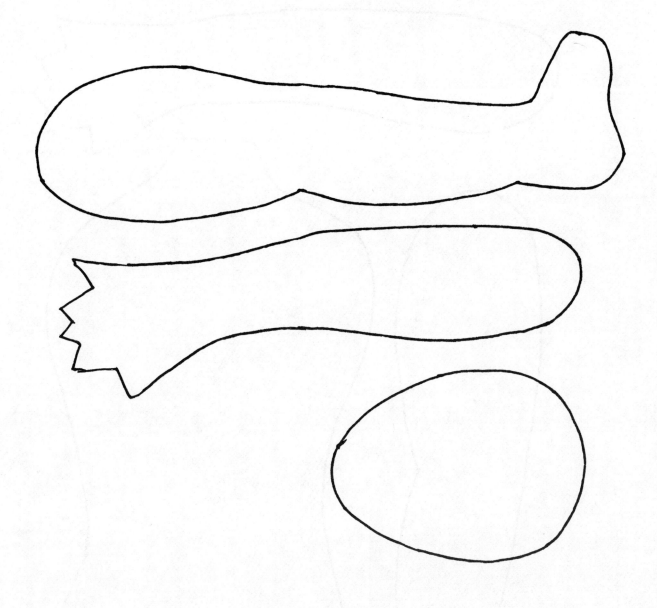

Cut out the body pieces. Arrange on the file folder as seen in the picture and trace around the outer edge. Encourage the child to place the body pieces correctly inside the body outline.

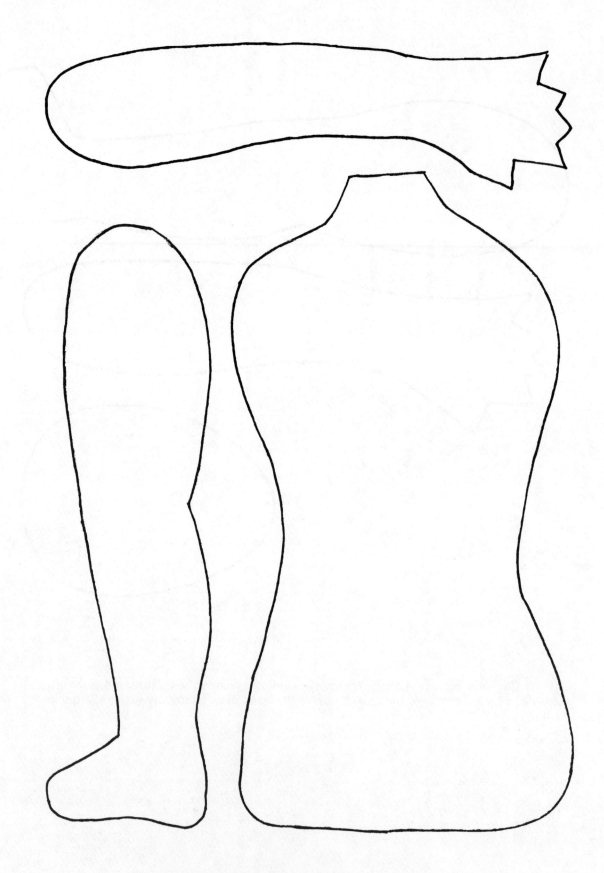

Identifies Familiar Objects

Can identify requested item from selection of three familiar toys.

DEVELOPMENTAL SIGNIFICANCE:

The child has to recognize differences between a set of items. At one level the child discriminates on the basis of shape — at another level on the basis of color.

TASK DESCRIPTION:

Place three items in front of the child and ask him to identify a specific item.

SAMPLE OBJECTIVE:

To identify a specific object from a set of similar or dissimilar objects.

SUGGESTED ACTIVITIES:

1. Place three familiar toys or shapes together. Ask the child to select one of them. Samples could include doll, car, and blocks or geometric shapes.

2. For a more advanced level, place three similiar, but differently colored objects together. Ask the child to select a particular colored object. Sponges can be cut into a variety of shapes, such as the fish below. Permanent magic markers can indicate eyes, mouth, etc. They can then be used in related water play.

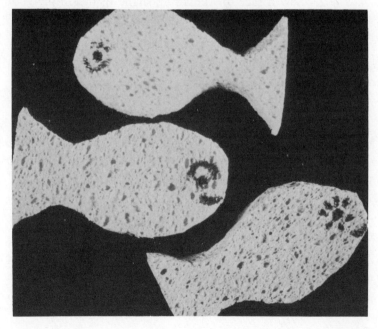

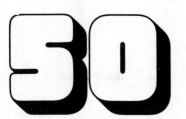

Recognizes Shapes

Fits circle, square, and triangle shape into holes of the same shape.

DEVELOPMENTAL SIGNIFICANCE:

The child recognizes that three types of geometric shapes can be labeled as squares, triangles or circles.

TASK DESCRIPTION:

The child will play with various shapes and learn to place them in corresponding holes.

SAMPLE OBJECTIVE:

To familiarize the child with basic geometric forms.

SUGGESTED ACTIVITIES:

1. Cut out two shapes of sturdy materials such as heavy cotton, felt, etc. Sew around the edge leaving a small space to stuff. Stuff it and finish stitching. Make several of different shapes. Cut out corresponding shapes on a large cardboard box. The baby will learn to place the stuffed shape into its appropriate hole.

2. Sew a face on the circle shape using simple geometric forms and attach to sides or crib or playpin. Exposure to the shapes will encourage identification.

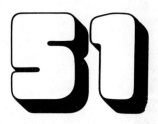

Understands Quantity

Knows concept of quantity, one and more than one.

DEVELOPMENTAL SIGNIFICANCE:

Identifying one or more than one object is an important prerequisite to counting and the awareness of amount. Familiar pictures or objects will make this task more relevant to the child.

TASK DESCRIPTION:

Provide experiences in counting for the child.

SAMPLE OBJECTIVE:

To learn number quantity.

SUGGESTED ACTIVITIES:

1. Mount pictures of familiar objects on colored paper. Cover them with clear contact paper. Tie the papers together with yarn or ribbon. Point to and name the picture. Then count how many objects are in the picture.

2. Cover the inside lid of a box with felt. Cut out numerous shapes of geometric forms. Place small felt shapes into sets on the lid of the box and count them with the child. A pipe cleaner can be used to circle the sets.

3. Place felt shapes in sets of one and more than one. Encourage the child to match the corresponding shapes, counting as he places them.

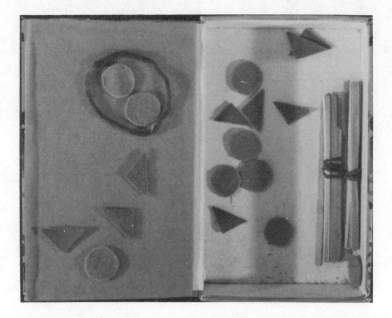

Item 51, SUGGESTED ACTIVITY 1.

Matches Objects

Can pick a matching object from a group of three objects when told, "Show me one like this."

DEVELOPMENTAL SIGNIFICANCE:

This will help the child increase his visual discrimination. Being able to recognize similar objects is a beginning step in reading readiness.

TASK DESCRIPTION:

Provide matching experiences for the child with buttons, cards or other tangible objects.

SAMPLE OBJECTIVE:

To increase visual awareness.

SUGGESTED ACTIVITIES:

1. Sew buttons on a file folder in the following manner: five buttons on the left column and five similar buttons on the rights column. Tie a string around the buttons on the left column. The child can take the string from one button and match to the correct button.

2. Glue various playing cards with different designs to a file folder. Provide the child with the same cards, but loose. Have him match the two cards.

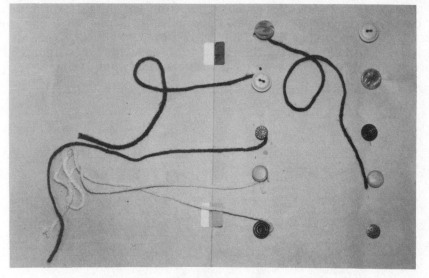

53

Works Puzzle

Works a 3—4 piece puzzle.

DEVELOPMENTAL SIGNIFICANCE:

Puzzles develop perceptual and problem solving abilities in the child and serve as a stimulation to learning. Children explore and experiment with puzzles, thus enhancing cognitive and conceptual growth. Children develop social relationships and share the materials with others. They learn to take turns and ask for what they want, which stimulates language growth. Puzzles also prepare the child for the highly motivational and independent format of the reading comprehension experience.

TASK DESCRIPTION:

Present puzzles as enjoyable games and demonstrate how the pieces are placed. Be sure to encourage the child to complete one puzzle before starting another and praise the child's successes.

SAMPLE OBJECTIVE:

To develop eye—hand coordination, fine motor development, recognition of shapes and colors, use of visual memory, form and generalizations.

SUGGESTED ACTIVITIES:

Puzzles should be large and of few pieces. Wooden or hard plastic puzzles are best. However, simple, inexpensive puzzles can be made from the child's favorite pictures. Cover their cereal box in clear contact paper and cut into pieces. He'll play with this puzzle over and over. Remember that children like to repeat activities that are reassuring. Practicing on known things lays the foundation for learning new things. Let the child practice on simple puzzles even after he has mastered complex ones.

Discriminates Size

Discriminates size: big and small, long and short.

DEVELOPMENTAL SIGNIFICANCE:

This will provide experiences for the child to develop concepts of size — a beginning math concept. He must understand size before numbers have any meaning.

TASK DESCRIPTION:

The child will learn to put smaller objects inside of larger ones.

SAMPLE OBJECTIVE:

To begin to build concepts of size and quantity (bigger and smaller, more and less).
To increase small muscle coordination.

SUGGESTED ACTIVITIES:

1. Assemble materials: three cans of different sizes (you may cover them with colorful contact paper); different sized boxes. Sit the baby on the floor and sit across from her. Show her a can, then show her a larger can. Place the smaller can into the larger can. Give her the can and encourage her to do the same. Stress the concepts of bigger and smaller and always praise the child for her efforts.

2. Repeat the experience in activity one with boxes. Increase the number of boxes.

Chapter 7
Humanics National Child Assessment Form: Motor Skills Development

MOTOR SKILLS DEVELOPMENT

As the child learns what his body can do, he learns about himself and his environment. The child must have the opportunity to develop his body skills. He will acquire a positive self-concept through participating successfully in movement activities. The infant is born with all the structures necessary for motor control, but the ability to control muscles and movement comes only with maturity and experience.

The body grows rapidly from birth to age two. The child needs special help in developing his skills during this period. Three types of skills should be taught to the young child.

Locomotor — Skills used to move the body from one place to another. Examples are crawling, walking, running, hopping, jumping, and climbing.

Nonlocomotor — Skills the child does in place. Examples are standing, twisting, shaking, bending, pushing, reaching and balancing.

Manipulative — Skills the child uses when he handles some kind of play object. Eye-hand coordination is enhanced as he reaches, grasps, and manipulates an object. Examples are playing with balls, beanbags, and blocks. The baby progresses from reaching for an object to swiping at it to grasping and finally manipulating it.

Gross Motor Skills

Gross motor skills are those involving the large muscles of the body. The use of the arms and legs, such as in walking and hitting, are examples. These large muscles are more developed during the early years. Therefore, the young child is more skillful in large movement activities than in fine motor activities. Gross motor skills using arms, legs, and torso are indicated on the CDAF.

Fine Motor Skills

Fine motor skills are those that utilize the small muscles of the body. The use of fingers, eyes, and toes are examples. These skills are much more difficult to master than the gross motor skills. The child must have the opportunity to use and develop these muscles. Activities that involve grasping, manipulating, stacking, and scribbling are noted on the CDAF.

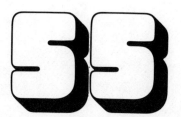 Holds Head And Chest Up

Holds head and chest up lying on stomach.

DEVELOPMENTAL SIGNIFICANCE:

This movement is part of a sequence of motor activities which results in crawling. At this stage the infant is developing particular strengths in the neck and chest.

TASK DESCRIPTION:

A rattle is used to attract the attention of the infant and encourage him to lift his head and chest in following its movement.

SAMPLE OBJECTIVE:

To give the infant experience in raising his neck and chest.

SUGGESTED ACTIVITIES:

1. Place the infant on his stomach and shake a rattle in front of him. Keep the rattle within the child's vision and experiment using it at slightly different heights. If the infant is stimulated by the object, he will tend to raise his head in order to maintain eye contact. Use a musical mobile for the same purpose.

2. Write your own activity.

Rolls To Side

Rolls from back to side.

DEVELOPMENTAL SIGNIFICANCE:

The infant progresses from kicking feet, wiggling and waving hands and looking from side to side while on his back, to attempted rolls. The first level is movement from back to side. This is followed by a complete roll from back to stomach. Rolls from stomach to back may be later developments.

TASK DESCRIPTION:

A rattle or bell are used to encourage the infant to roll from back to side.

SAMPLE OBJECTIVE:

To encourage the child to roll to his side or onto his stomach.

SUGGESTED ACTIVITIES:

1. While the child is lying on his back, show him a rattle or bell. Ring the bell and let the child's eyes follow it to a resting place at his side. Give encouragement to him to reach out for it. It should be placed a little beyond the reach of the child to encourage him to roll onto his side to retrieve it.

2. Write your own activity.

 Swipes

Swipes at hanging objects.

DEVELOPMENTAL SIGNIFICANCE:

As the child becomes more aware of objects in his environment, he will attempt to reach out and touch them. Batting or swiping at hanging objects is a prerequisite stage to actually grabbing and holding them. Becoming aware of hands and feet and grabbing a foot to place in his mouth are also part of this developmental period.

TASK DESCRIPTION:

The child is given mobiles to swipe at while lying on his back in a crib.

SAMPLE OBJECTIVE:

To encourage the child to touch and hold mobiles in a crib.

SUGGESTED ACTIVITIES:

1. String a collection of large colorful plastic toys across crib or playpen just within reach of the child. Divert the attention of the infant to them by turning or shaking them gently. Encourage the child to reach for these toys and give verbal praise when he successfully bats or holds one of them.

2. Write your own activity.

 Crawls

Crawls on stomach.

DEVELOPMENTAL SIGNIFICANCE:

As the infant becomes more aware of his world, he begins to explore it by creeping from place to place. This action enables the child to use his hands and feet to push himself along on his stomach. Rocking backwards and forwards on hands and knees and subsequently crawling on them may replace the stomach crawl in some infants. Others creep on all fours without using the knees. A few children never creep or crawl — they omit this stage and begin walking.

TASK DESCRIPTION:

An object is placed slightly out of reach of the child and he is prompted to creep towards it.

SAMPLE OBJECTIVE:

To provide the child with a stimulus to encourage him to creep or crawl from one point to another.

SUGGESTED ACTIVITIES:

1. Place the infant on his stomach and sit a short distance in front of him holding one of his favorite toys. Show him the toy and give him the verbal encouragement to come and get it. Alternatively, simply place the favored object in front of the child so that he has to creep forward to reach it.

2. Write your own activity.

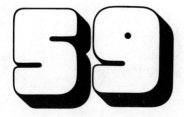 Holds Bottle

Holds bottle while being fed.

DEVELOPMENTAL SIGNIFICANCE:

As the child becomes more expert in using his hands, he moves from merely slapping at objects to holding them. A feeding bottle is of primary interest and the infant can be expected to hold one with one or both hands while being fed.

TASK DESCRIPTION:

Feed the child using a bottle.

SAMPLE OBJECTIVE:

To encourage the child to hold the feeding bottle.

SUGGESTED ACTIVITIES:

1. When feeding the child with a bottle, encourage him to hold it with one or both hands. If the child does not hold the bottle voluntarily, place his hands on it and place your hands over his.

2. Write your own activity.

 **Turns Body**

From sitting position, turns body in response to to rattling toy.

DEVELOPMENTAL SIGNIFICANCE:

Sitting, rolling and creeping movements occur at similar times, although the infant may be more expert in one activity than another. As the child becomes more adept at total bodily coordination, and begins to explore his world, he will try to sit up. Assistance and support are needed at first, but the child will rapidly develop the ability to sit alone.

TASK DESCRIPTION:

The child will turn his body to look at an object in response to an auditory stimulus.

SAMPLE OBJECTIVE:

To motivate the child to turn his head and body in response to a rattling toy.

SUGGESTED ACTIVITIES:

1. When the child is able to sit up unassisted, show him a rattle, bell or other toy that makes an attracting sound. Shake it in front of him and then slowly move it from side to side so that the child needs to turn to see it.

2. Write your own activity.

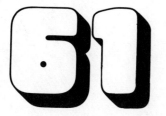

Crawls After Ball

Moves a ball and crawls after it.

DEVELOPMENTAL SIGNIFICANCE:

This stage brings together the interest of the infant in touching objects in the environment and his increasing ability in crawling.

TASK DESCRIPTION:

The child is given a large ball to push and crawl after.

SAMPLE OBJECTIVE:

The child will crawl towards a ball, move it forward, and continue to pursue it.

SUGGESTED ACTIVITIES:

1. When the child is able to crawl unassisted, show him a ball. Hold it in front of him and then place it on the ground. Encourage him to reach and crawl after the ball.

2. Write your own activity.

Pulls up

Pulls self to standing position.

DEVELOPMENTAL SIGNIFICANCE:

The ability to move from a sitting or crawling position to standing is a necessary aspect of getting ready to walk. It is also part of a continuing process through which the child expands his experiences with his environment. Initially, the infant may pull himself up successfully, but may require help in returning to a sitting position.

TASK DESCRIPTION:

The child will be placed in a crib or playpen or next to a soft cushioned piece of furniture and be encouraged to pull himself up to touch objects that he wants.

SAMPLE OBJECTIVE:

The child will be encouraged to pull himself up into a standing position.

SUGGESTED ACTIVITIES:

1. String toys around the top of a crib or playpen. Encourage the child to pull himself up using the bars or netting to reach them. Alternatively, place favored toys on a sofa or soft arm chair and tell the child to stand up or pull up to get them. Forcing or hurrying the child into this activity is not desirable. It is to be encouraged when the infant shows readiness for it.

2. Write your own activity.

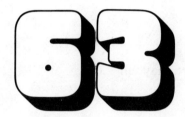

Walks With Support

Walks while hands are held or holding to furniture.

DEVELOPMENTAL SIGNIFICANCE:

This is an intermediate step between the child's ability to pull himself up into a standing position and walking without assistance. It is important not to force development. Some children who are heavy may be late in mastering this process. Others may be bowlegged which indicates that their legs have not straightened out. Some may not have developed the muscular strength in their legs to permit much movement beyond the standing position.

TASK DESCRIPTION:

Provide a hazard free environment which the child can explore by holding on to objects for support.

SAMPLE OBJECTIVE:

The child will move around a playpen or room holding on to bars or furniture for support.

SUGGESTED ACTIVITIES:

1. Provide a crib, playpen or use a regular room in which the child can hold on to solid objects as he explores his environment.

2. Hold both hands of the infant as he attempts to walk from place to place. Keep this activity up for short periods of time.

Walks Without Support

Walks forward without support, may fall occasionally.

DEVELOPMENTAL SIGNIFICANCE:

The child will naturally reach a point when he can take a step or two without support. A good deal of falling may occur until this ability is developed.

TASK DESCRIPTION:

Take a walk with the child.

SAMPLE OBJECTIVE:

To use large muscles and develop increasing skill in walking. Combine this activity with further sensory experiences in the child's environment.

SUGGESTED ACTIVITIES:

1. Set aside as much time as possible to walk with the child. Plan a walk with activities that will use the senses of sight, sound and touch. Listen to the birds, an airplane, or a siren. Feel the sun or wind or the rough bark on a tree.

2. Continue taking the walk and allow the child to collect things such as sticks or rocks.

3. Use other senses on the walk: smell the air or walk barefoot and feel the ground.

 Squats

Squats down and stands back up without support.

DEVELOPMENTAL SIGNIFICANCE:

The child shows increasing competence in maintaining control over his whole body. Use of the squat position develops after skills in balancing on two feet and walking have been achieved.

TASK DESCRIPTION:

Provide a model for the child to imitate the squat position using games and dramatic activities.

SAMPLE OBJECTIVE:

To provide opportunities for the child to use the squat position.

SUGGESTED ACTIVITIES:

1. Place some interesting toys on the floor in front of the child and ask him to reach down and retrieve them by squatting and then standing back up. Demonstrate how to do this as necessary.

2. Play a game in which the child stretches up to be as tall as he can and then slowly becomes smaller and smaller until he makes a small tight shape in the squat position.

3. Fill a large bowl or baby bath with floating objects. Encourage the child to squat at the side of the container to *fish out* the floating items.

 Walks Backward

Walks backward.

DEVELOPMENTAL SIGNIFICANCE:

At this level the child has already mastered the prerequisite skills for walking backwards outlined in items 63 and 65. He is now more confident in moving, has more control, and an increased understanding of himself in relation to the space around him.

TASK DESCRIPTION:

Combine dramatic activities and movement experiences in enhancing competence in walking backwards.

SAMPLE OBJECTIVE:

To help the child gain self-confidence by gaining further self-control of his body.

SUGGESTED ACTIVITIES:

1. Take the child by the hand and slowly walk backward for a few feet. It may be difficult for him at first, but he'll enjoy keeping up with you. Praise him for his efforts.

2. Pretend to be a car or a train which moves forwards and backwards. Make the sound of each machine to accompany the action. Do this while holding hands with the child and subsequently at the independent level where the hands are released.

3. Make a game of walking forward from one piece of furniture to another and then walking backwards between them. Increase the distance between objects as confidence grows.

 **67** Carries Large Object

Carries a large object (such as a large ball
ball) while walking.

DEVELOPMENTAL SIGNIFICANCE:

The ability to carry an object while walking illustrates that the child can maintain his footing and balance without using his arms for extension. It combines
earlier learnings in which the child has achieved skills in holding and moving objects with new skills in walking.

TASK DESCRIPTION:

Use a stuffed animal made by the parent or teacher to promote walking and
carrying activities.

SAMPLE OBJECTIVE:

To combine walking and carrying skills.

SUGGESTED ACTIVITIES:

Make a large stuffed animal for the child by following these directions. Cut out
two circles from scrap material (washable), eight tube-shaped pieces of material,
and eyes, nose, and mouth from felt. Sew face features on each side of the circle. Stitch the circles together inside out leaving a small opening at the top.
Fill with cotton. Stuff and sew on the legs. Do not use buttons or items that
can be chewed off. Use this animal and similar toys to practice the objective.

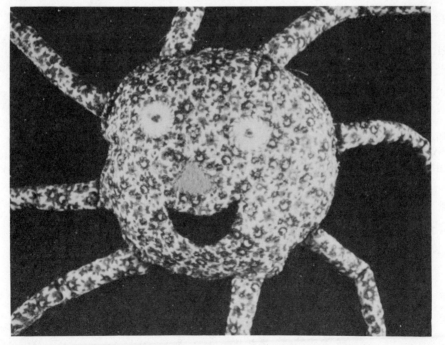

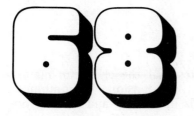

Kicks Ball

Kicks a ball with one foot.

DEVELOPMENTAL SIGNIFICANCE:

In order to kick a ball the child must balance briefly on one leg. The ability to do this demonstrates a higher level of balance than walking and squatting and also shows the child that he can move an object with his feet.

TASK DESCRIPTION:

Use a ball, empty plastic milk container or large plastic bowl to practice kicking.

SAMPLE OBJECTIVE:

To learn how to balance momentarily on one foot while kicking a ball with the other.

SUGGESTED ACTIVITIES:

1. Hold the hand of the child while he kicks at a lightweight ball. When the activity is mastered, encourage him to kick the ball without assistance.

2. Place several empty plastic milk jugs in a row. Put the ball in front of them. Have the child kick the ball so that it bumps the containers.

3. Play the same game noted under Number 2 with large plastic skittles. Encourage the child to squat down and put the skittles back up after he has hit them with the ball. This will reinforce the ability to squat noted earlier.

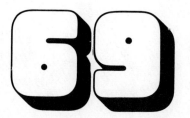

Jumps In Place

Jumps in place with both feet.

DEVELOPMENTAL SIGNIFICANCE:

In the kicking activity the child practiced momentary balance on one foot. At this stage both feet leave the ground for an instant. It represents a level of increased coordination, security in movement, and refines control of the whole body.

TASK DESCRIPTION:

Practice jumping in place using both feet with a sound stimulus or a jump rope to help.

SAMPLE OBJECTIVE:

To practice two-footed jumps.

SUGGESTED ACTIVITIES:

1. Show the child a two-footed jump and ask him to copy it.

2. Add to the activity by using a pot or drum. Jump at the beat of the drum.

3. Practice tiny jumps and then try to jump higher.

4. Later on, place a jump rope on the floor and have the child practice jumping over it using a two-footed jump.

 Balances On One Foot

Stands on one foot at a time with help.

DEVELOPMENTAL SIGNIFICANCE:

This is a further refinement of motor coordination which builds on earlier learnings related to balance.

TASK DESCRIPTION:

The child imitates balancing on one foot and subsequently plays *Simon Said* in order to practice the skill.

SAMPLE OBJECTIVE:

To balance on one foot.

SUGGESTED ACTIVITIES:

1. Show the child how to balance on one foot. Practice the activity while holding his hand, and subsequently without offering assistance.

2. Modify the traditional game of *Simon Said* to include balancing on one foot, walking forwards and backwards, squatting and jumping.

3. Practice a game called *Walking Tall* in which the child raises one leg as high as possible, puts it down and then repeats the action with the other leg.

 Rides Tricycle

Rides a tricycle.

DEVELOPMENTAL SIGNIFICANCE:

This skill requires that legs and feet are moved in a coordinated fashion. It builds on earlier levels of coordination stressing balance on one foot or the other and two-footed jumps.

TASK DESCRIPTION:

Practice coordination of legs and feet by allowing the child to ride a tricycle.

SAMPLE OBJECTIVE:

To coordinate leg and feet movements to move a tricycle forward.

SUGGESTED ACTIVITY:

Sit the child on a small tricycle. Make sure that his feet can easily touch the pedals. Place your hands on the child's feet and pedals and move them in such a way that the tricycle moves towards you. Push the tricycle back and practice the activity again. Tell the child how his feet are pushing the tricycle along. Allow him to practice the activity independently.

Walks On Tiptoes

Walks five steps on tiptoes.

DEVELOPMENTAL SIGNIFICANCE:

This item reinforces earlier balancing activities, but adds a refinement of balancing on the toes rather than the feet. It requires the use of additional leg muscles and represents a different way of moving the whole body.

TASK DESCRIPTION:

Improvised dances and dramatic activities are used to promote movement on tiptoes.

SAMPLE OBJECTIVE:

To practice balancing on tiptoes.

SUGGESTED ACTIVITIES:

1. Practice simply walking a few steps on tiptoes. Add to the activity by moving to a slow musical accompaniment.

2. Use the idea of being a high flying bird, a ballet dancer, or a leaf blown high by the wind in order to reach and stretch up tall while moving.

3. Practice reaching for objects which are placed at increasing heights so that the child has to stand on tiptoes to reach them.

 Holds Rattle

Holds a rattle placed in hand.

DEVELOPMENTAL SIGNIFICANCE:

The child advances from an ability to manipulate and carry large objects to similar competence with smaller items. Coordination improves from gross motor learnings to fine motor coordination.

TASK DESCRIPTION:

The child is able to hold and manipulate a rattle placed in his hand.

SAMPLE OBJECTIVE:

To develop fine motor skills through holding a small toy.

SUGGESTED ACTIVITIES:

1. Practice holding the rattle and shaking it in a variety of ways. Make quiet sounds and noisy sounds. Try to shake the rattle to match a simple count or rhythm.

2. Identify a range of small objects for the child to hold and manipulate, such as a drumstick or beater to a musical triangle.

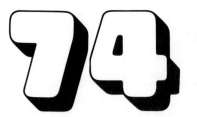

Follows Moving Object (I)

Eyes and head follow side to side motion of an object. (Child lying on back.)

DEVELOPMENTAL SIGNIFICANCE:

The child develops the ability to move the eyes and head in order to follow an object. This eye focus indicates the interest of the child in moving objects in his environment and may be a prerequisite skill to later work requiring hand—eye coordination.

TASK DESCRIPTION:

Show the child a variety of toys and move them from side to side, encouraging him to watch them.

SAMPLE OBJECTIVE:

To encourage the child to follow a moving object where the eyes and head follow the object from side to side.

SUGGESTED ACTIVITIES:

1. When the child is lying on his back, show him a favorite toy. Move it from side to side. Talk about the movement of the toy. Encourage him to watch where it goes.

2. Write your own activity.

 Follows Moving Object (II)

Eyes and head follow an object moved from above eyes to behind head. (Child lying on back.)

DEVELOPMENTAL SIGNIFICANCE:

This requires increased concentration and more refined eye focus. It builds on Item 75.

TASK DESCRIPTION:

Move favorite toys or interesting objects in a range of directions encouraging the child to follow the movement with his eyes.

SAMPLE OBJECTIVE:

To diversify coordinated eye-head movements from side to side movements to more complicated levels.

SUGGESTED ACTIVITIES:

1. Show the child a favorite toy. Move it from side to side and then above and behind the child. Tell him to keep looking at it or for it. Talk about the movement of it throughout the activity.

2. Write your own activity.

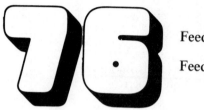

Feeds Self

Feeds self cracker or teething biscuit.

DEVELOPMENTAL SIGNIFICANCE:

This action combines holding small objects (Number 73) with eye focus (Number 74 and 75) into a coordinated movement requiring both hand and eye coordination.

TASK DESCRIPTION:

Give the child a cracker or teething biscuit and let him eat it.

SAMPLE OBJECTIVE:

To encourage hand and eye coordination through a simple feeding activity.

SUGGESTED ACTIVITIES:

1. Place a cracker or biscuit in the hand of the child. Encourage him to eat it. Note: As small children explore their worlds through their senses they put many things into their mouths. It is an almost automatic response to suck on toys and foodstuffs.

2. Write your own activity.

 Exchanges Object Between Hands

Passes object from one hand to another.

DEVELOPMENTAL SIGNIFICANCE:

This action is a refinement of earlier developments where the child is seen to hold an object with both hands or with one hand. The movement also builds an increasing level of performance in eye-hand coordination.

TASK DESCRIPTION:

Practice eye-hand coordination.

SAMPLE OBJECTIVE:

To pass a toy or other item from one hand to the other.

SUGGESTED ACTIVITIES:

1. Hold a toy in one hand and pass it to the other. Ask the child to follow the the activity and imitate your actions.

2. Write your own activity.

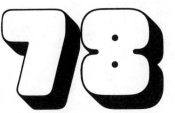 Picks Up Block

Picks up a one-inch block.

DEVELOPMENTAL SIGNIFICANCE:

Being able to pick up a block is a prerequisite to other fine motor development skills. The child will show interest in blocks and thus want to manipulate them for his entertainment. Later he will be able to stack them and create structures.

TASK DESCRIPTION:

Practicing eye-hand coordination, learning how to imitate.

SAMPLE OBJECTIVE:

To pick up a block in each hand.

SUGGESTED ACTIVITIES:

1. Cover different sizes of milk cartons with contact paper. Sit the baby on the floor and sit across from him. The infant can pick up and hold the blocks. He can imitate your actions. Say, "I picked up a block. You can pick one up, too." Encourage him to pick up the blocks.

2. Write your own activity.

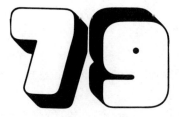 Brings Objects Together

Bangs two blocks together, one in each hand.

DEVELOPMENTAL SIGNIFICANCE:

This development in fine motor coordination brings together earlier skills in which the child has practiced picking up items and moving them from one hand to the other.

TASK DESCRIPTION:

Encourage the child to pick up two blocks and hit them against each other.

SAMPLE OBJECTIVE:

To foster increased development of fine motor skills and eye-hand coordination.

SUGGESTED ACTIVITIES:

1. Cover a number of small light weight containers with contact paper to make them attractive to the child. Encourage the child to pick them up with two hands and then hold one in each hand. Show him how he can make a sound by hitting the boxes together.

2. Add to the interest of the activity by placing objects within the boxes or containers so that they make a variety of sounds when brought together.

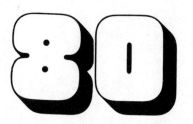 **Puts Objects Into Container**

Puts small objects through a slot into a container.

DEVELOPMENTAL SIGNIFICANCE:

The child not only picks up objects which requres fine motor coordination, but is able to transfer them from one location to another.

TASK DESCRIPTION:

Allow the child to fill a container with small objects.

SAMPLE OBJECTIVE:

To practice eye-hand coordination and help the infant to learn to follow directions.

SUGGESTED ACTIVITIES:

1. Cover a box (an oatmeal box is pictured) with colorful contact paper. Put safe objects next to the box. Suggested objects could be a jar lid, bell, clothes pin, and measuring spoons. Make a slit in the box lid. The child can put the objects into the container.

2. Put a muffin tray or egg carton and small objects that fit into the containers in front of the child. Be sure the objects are not too small that they can be swallowed. Encourage the child to place the objects into the containers.

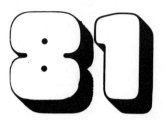

Grasps Tiny Object

Grasps raisin or other tiny object with thumb and forefinger.

DEVELOPMENTAL SIGNIFICANCE:

In this instance, fine motor coordination increases from use of the whole hand or several fingers, to the use of only two of them. (The thumb and forefinger are usually used.)

TASK DESCRIPTION:

Allow the child to pick up tiny portions of food or small objects and eat them or play with them as the object suggests.

SAMPLE OBJECTIVE:

To pick up small items with the thumb and forefinger.

SUGGESTED ACTIVITIES:

1. Place the child on the floor or in a high chair. Place a few raisins in front of him. The child will grasp them and place them in his mouth.

2. Let the child pick up some small cookie cutters and try to press their shape into a piece of soft clay or similar material.

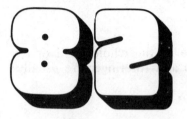 **Fits Ring Onto Peg**

Fits a 2"-4" ring onto a peg.

DEVELOPMENTAL SIGNIFICANCE:

This level relates back to skills which require picking up small objects (Number 81) and moving them from one place to another (Number 80). In this instance, the skill is more precise in that an object of specified shape has to be placed over another object. More attention to hand-eye coordination is required.

TASK DESCRIPTION:

The child will play with pegs and rings and place one over the other.

SAMPLE OBJECTIVE:

To place a ring over a peg in order to foster more precise eye-hand coordination.

SUGGESTED ACTIVITIES:

1. Buy or make a simple ring and peg set and show the child how the ring fits over the peg. Let him experiment with it.

2. Later, use a ring and peg set in which the rings and pegs are graduated in size. At first, practice putting on the largest two rings. Add additional rings as competence increases.

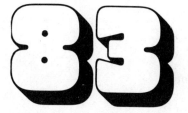 Drinks From Cup

Drinks from a cup or glass without help,
may spill occasionally.

DEVELOPMENTAL SIGNIFICANCE:

This gives the child an opportunity to refine skills. The acts of eating and drinking are of immediate interest to the child. Earlier experiences and knowledge are required to accomplish this task.

TASK DESCRIPTION:

Allow the child to drink from a cup without assistance.

SAMPLE OBJECTIVE:

To further enhance fine motor skills.

SUGGESTED ACTIVITIES:

1. Give the child a baby cup with a weighted bottom containing his favorite beverage. Allow him to experiment with drinking from it. Anticipate some spills and attempt to ignore them.

2. Write your own activity.

 **Brings Spoon To Food**

Holds a spoon and dips into food.

DEVELOPMENTAL SIGNIFICANCE:

The child is given an opportunity to feed himself using knowledge and experiences learned earlier. This is a continuation of Item 83.

TASK DESCRIPTION:

Allow the child to hold a spoon and try to feed himself.

SAMPLE OBJECTIVE:

To enhance fine motor development.

SUGGESTED ACTIVITIES:

1. Provide a dish of mashed potatoes or squashed vegetables in a dish. Give the child an opportunity to experiment with a spoon in an attempt to feed himself.

2. Write your own activity.

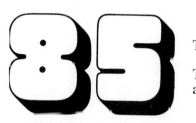

Turns Pages

Turns pages of a book, maybe several at a time.

DEVELOPMENTAL SIGNIFICANCE:

Movement and Directionality are related skills. Turning the pages of a book can be seen as an offshoot of earlier actions requiring careful manipulation, fine motor performance and continuing attention to hand-eye coordination.

TASK DESCRIPTION:

Encourage the child to turn pages or strum a guitar to encourage motor coordination.

SAMPLE OBJECTIVE:

To look at a book together.

SUGGESTED ACTIVITIES:

1. Sit in a comfortable chair with the infant in your lap. Show him a book which has large simple pictures. Show him how to turn the pages and tell him about the pictures. His interest span may only be a few minutes.

2. An alternative activity which requires a similar movement to that of turning pages is strumming guitar strings. A shoe box can be covered with contact paper and a hole can be cut in the top, as pictured. Rubber bands can be stretched over the box.

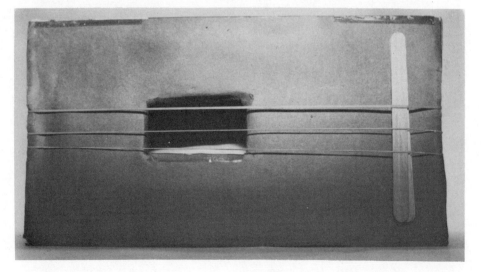

 Stacks Blocks (I)

Stacks a tower of four one-inch blocks.

DEVELOPMENTAL SIGNIFICANCE:

After the child has practiced picking up blocks (Item 78) and bringing them together (Item 79), he may be ready to place them on top of one another. This is a fine motor, hand-eye and spatial activity.

TASK DESCRIPTION:

Give the child four one inch blocks and provide ample time for picking them up and stacking them.

SAMPLE OBJECTIVE:

To practice stacking blocks.

SUGGESTED ACTIVITIES:

1. Obtain a set of blocks such as those developed by the Educational Division of Reader's Digest. (Reader's Digest Services, Inc./Educational Division, Pleasantville, New York 10570). For initial action, use large blocks for stacking. Subsequently, use smaller blocks to match developmental skill level.

2. Write your own activity.

Scribbles

Stays on large paper while scribbling.

DEVELOPMENTAL SIGNIFICANCE:

The first stages of artistic development, according to Viktor Lowenfeld, a noted art educator, is encompassed by this task and is identified as the *scribbling stage*.

TASK DESCRIPTION:

Provide the child with a large sheet of paper and crayons.

SAMPLE OBJECTIVE:

To practice scribbling using small muscles. Good control of the hands is necessary before learning to write.

SUGGESTED ACTIVITIES:

1. Provide the child with the following materials: paper, crayon, pencil, magic markers and several simple objects such as cans and blocks.

   First allow the child to use any of the drawing instruments and scribble on his paper.

2. For a later task, help the child trace around one on the objects. Help hold the object on the paper to keep it from slipping. Then help the child trace around the object and show her how the shape she drew is similar to the object. Don't worry if the shape is not very clear. It may be just a scribble, but the effort will improve as she gains more control.

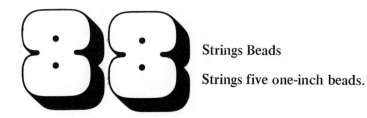 Strings Beads

Strings five one-inch beads.

DEVELOPMENTAL SIGNIFICANCE:

This represents a further level of development of fine motor activity which follows moving objects into a container (Item 80) and placing rings over a peg (Item 82).

TASK DESCRIPTION:

Provide rings made of play dough and shoe strings for the child to practice the activity.

SAMPLE OBJECTIVE:

To learn to string beads.

SUGGESTED ACTIVITY:

Use the following recipe to make salt ceramic one inch beads.

1 cup salt
1/2 cup cornstarch
3/4 cup cold water

Mix salt and cornstarch and grad-
ually add cold water. Do this in
the top of a double boiler until the
consistency of bread dough is achieved.
Makes enough for one set of beads.

Ask the child to thread the beads using a shoe string.

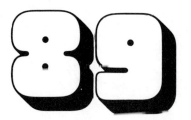

Stacks Blocks (II)

Stacks a tower of eight one-inch blocks.

DEVELOPMENTAL SIGNIFICANCE:

This activity is similar to Item 86, except the child will stack eight instead of four one-inch blocks.

TASK DESCRIPTION:

Give the child eight one-inch blocks and provide ample time for picking them up and stacking them.

SAMPLE OBJECTIVE:

To practice stacking blocks.

SUGGESTED ACTIVITIES:

1. Obtain a set of blocks and put them on the floor in front of the child. Help him build towers of blocks.

2. Encourage the child to create architectural forms. Tunnels, ramps and grids can be constructed. As the child becomes more advanced in his block building, he becomes aware of concepts such as leverage, balance and stability. Eye-hand coordination and perception are strengthened. Feelings of accomplishment result.

   Provide a variety of blocks as pictured.

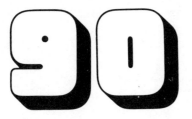

90 Unbuttons Buttons

Unbuttons large buttons.

DEVELOPMENTAL SIGNIFICANCE:

This is a continuing aspect of fine motor development. It requires close attention to coordination and builds on all previous learning tasks.

TASK DESCRIPTION:

Given a doll with buttons or similar piece of equipment, the child practices unbuttoning buttons.

SAMPLE OBJECTIVE:

To provide activities with unbuttoning buttons and related actions.

SUGGESTED ACTIVITIES:

1. Make a dressing board as shown. Include buttons, laces and zippers. Practice undoing them in turn.

2. Use a commercially produced doll such as *Dressy Betsy* or *Dapper Dan*, (Playskool, Inc., Chicago, Illinois). These dolls are specifically designed to teach or reinforce this skill.

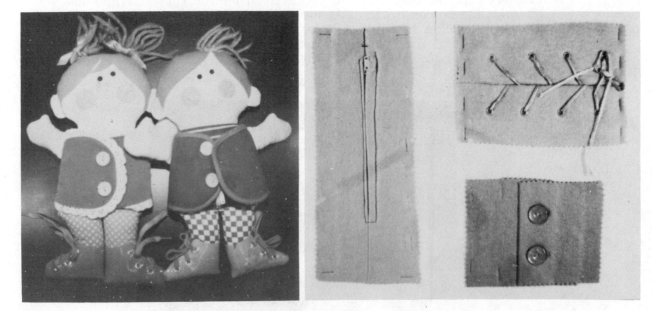

Chapter 8
Using the results of The Humanics National Child Assessment Form

Once the Humanics National Child Assessment Form has been administered, the results must be used in planning appropriate learning experiences for the child. Otherwise there is little reason for administering the HNCAF. The profile on the back of the HNCAF will show you at a glance which skills the child has mastered and which ones you can provide learning experiences for.

This chapter will show how to use the results of the HNCAF in developing an educational plan. The sample show the completed HNCAF on one child, Lara, and how to select appropriate activities for her.

The Individualized Educational Program

The first step is to administer the HNCAF to determine what the child is able to do. The item number is reproduced on the IEP form.[*] Additional information, such as parent reports, can also be included on the IEP. Be sure and include an assessment of all four areas on the HNCAF. Remember, the child's behavior will develop in sequence, but the rate will vary. At a glance, the teacher can see the areas of strength of the child's abilities. You can see if he has developed more in one area or another. For example, has he only completed four items in Language, but nine items in Gross Motor? If so, the teacher and parent may want to spend more time in language activities with the child. These activities can be noted under **Annual Goals**.

The **Instructional Objectives** are short-term behavioral expectations. Sample objectives are found on the same page as the item number in Chapters 4-7. The teacher or parent will want to decide which activities he will provide. You will want to first provide activities that have been identified as **Appeared**. These skills are emerging, therefore they should be considered first. You should then go on to the next item (items) and plan activities accordingly. If you have gaps between items, plan activities to develop these skills. Remember the Suggested Activities in the manual only provide an idea. You may think of many more.

---

[*] The IEP form is available from Humanics Limited, P.O. Box 7447, Atlanta, Ga. 30309.

Monitoring the Child's Progress: When and How

In this area, the teacher should state how a child's gains will be evaluated. She should again refer to the objectives following the item numbers and state, in behavioral objectives, how she will determine if the child has accomplished a task. She should note when she will check this item.

Educational Program

Indicate the amount of time a child spends in the educational setting, such as full day, half day, or two days a week.

The date the IEP is initiated should be noted. The persons preparing the IEP should sign the form (teacher, parent, etc.)

On the following pages is a completed sample of Lara's HNCAF. The dates at the top of the form indicate the time spent giving the assessment. As items were administered, checks and dates were written in the appropriate space. At the bottom of the form are "Notes". Any information relating to her participation in the activities is noted. These results are included on the back of the form, the Child Development Summary Profile.

Lara's Social—Emotional Development

The CDS Profile has also been included on the IEP form. The Social—Emotional section reveals that items 1—7 have Occurred Consistently, while item 10 Occurs Occasionally. As explained earlier, the first items to plan activities for may be 8,9, and 11. Since the tasks are arranged developmentally, the teacher decided to stop the assessment at this point.

In developing the Goals and Objectives for Lara, it would seem appropriate that an objective and sample activity under item 8,9, and 11 would be selected.

It would also be necessary to monitor Lara's growth. After playing with the game or activity, it may be feasible to recheck Lara's ability to perform the task in about a month.

Lara's **Language Development**

The Language Development section reveals that items 19–25 have Occurred Consistently, while item 26 Occurs Occasionally. The items to plan activities for may be 26, 27, etc.

Again Sample Objectives and Suggested Activities are found below the item number. Language is such a vital area that the teacher and parent will want to spend as much time as possible in Language Development activities.

Language at this point in development will emerge slowly. Waiting at least one–two months would seem an adequate time to wait before reassessing the skill.

Lara's **Cognitive Growth**

Lara was able to respond consistently to items 37–41, 43, and 44, while items 45 and 46 Occur Occasionally.

Items to plan activities for should be 42, 45, and 46.

Reassessment should occur after Lara has had adequate opportunity to develop these skills.

Lara's **Motor Skills**

Lara seems to be developing well in her motor skills, especially Gross Motor. Items 55–64 have Occurred Consistently, while items 65–66 Occur Occasionally. Under Fine Motor Skills, items 73–83 Occur Consistently, while items 82–85 Occur Occasionally.

Activities to plan would involve items 65-67and 82-86.

The items Lara has occasionally achieved should be reinforced with ample opportunity and she should again be rechecked in due time.

Once the Individualized Educational Program has been developed, activities should be made and selected to help reach the planned objectives. It is up to you to decide what activities to make now for your children.

SUMMARY

The Child Development Assessment Form and this manual are presented for your use in assessing children from birth to age three. We suggest you continue this assessment process with the *Humanics National Preschool Assessment Handbook (Ages 3-6).*

We hope you found this process helpful to you and can make and adapt the activities for use with your children.

ADDITIONAL RESOURCES ON INFANTS AND TODDLERS

Ames, Louise B. YOUR TWO YEAR OLD and YOUR THREE YEAR OLD. New York: Delacorte, 1976.

Ault, Ruth L. CHILDREN'S COGNITIVE DEVELOPMENT: PIAGET'S THEORY AND THE PROCESS APPROACH. New York: Oxford University, 1977.

Biehler, Robert F. CHILD DEVELOPMENT: AN INTRODUCTION. Boston: Houghton-Mifflin, 1976.

Bower, T.G.R. A PRIMER OF INFANT DEVELOPMENT. San Francisco: W.H. Freeman and Co., 1977.

Cohen. Monroe. ed. UNDERSTANDING AND NURTURING INFANT DE-VELOPMENT, 1976 and DEVELOPING PROGRAMS FOR INFANTS AND TODDLERS. Washington, D.C.: Association for Childhood Education International.

Gesell, Arnold. THE FIRST FIVE YEARS OF LIFE. New York: Harper, 1974.

Gordon, Ira. BABY LEARNING THROUGH BABY PLAY. New York: St. Martin's Press, 1970.

Gordon, Ira. CHILD LEARNING THROUGH CHILD PLAY. New York: St. Martin's Press, 1972.

Jones, Sandy. GOOD THINGS FOR BABIES. Boston: Houghton-Mifflin, 1976.

Polokoff, Marion and Colleen Mayer. BABY'S LIB. Anchorage, AK: Alaska Special Services Project, 726 E. St., 99501. 1976.

Rowen, Betty. THE CHILDREN WE SEE. New York: Holt, Rinehart and Winston, Inc., 1973.

Segal, M. and Don Adcock. FROM ONE TO TWO YEARS. Rolling Hills Estates, CA, Winch and Asso., 1976.

Singer, Dorothy. PARTNERS IN PLAY: A STEP-BY-STEP GUIDE TO IMAG — INATIVE PLAY IN CHILDREN. New York: Harper, 1977.

Sutton-Smith, Brian. HOW TO PLAY WITH YOUR CHILDREN (AND WHEN NOT TO). New York: Hawthorne, 1974.

Humanics National Child Assessment Form
Birth to Three

Marsha Kaufman, Ph.D. and T. Thomas McMurrain, Ph.D.

Child's Name

Age   **Date of Birth**

Child Development Class

Teacher

Teacher Aide

Child Development Center

ABOUT THE FORM

The *Child Development Assessment Form* is a checklist of skills and behaviors a child is likely to develop from birth to three years of age. Each item in the checklist is a sample of many related skills and behaviors and in that sense serves as an index of more general characteristics of development. Items in the Assessment Form are grouped into five scales that represent areas of child development: **Social-Emotional, Language, Cognitive, Gross Motor** and **Fine Motor.**

Within each scale, the items are arranged in a developmental sequence, and space is provided for assessing the child three times during the year. The Child Development Profile allows a visual representation of the child's ratings on each scale at the time of each assessment.

A NOTE TO THE PARENT

No one knows more about the development of your child than you do. This checklist is to structure some topics you and the teacher will discuss about your child. You may often want to add your own opinions and observations about your child's development. The information you and the teacher share is very important in designing an educational experience which will respond to and stimulate the individual nature and personality of your child.

DIRECTIONS

Complete all the items in the Assessment Form by observing the child in everyday play activities, or, if necessary, structuring special situations to let you observe the described behavior.

Mark each item as follows:

Make No Check Mark –	If the characteristic is not present or the behavior does not occur.
Check in the "Occurs Occasionally" Column –	If the characteristic or behavior is sometimes present, but is not a consistent part of the behavior. The behavior has occurred occasionally but is not firmly mastered or developed.
Check in the "Occurs Consistently" Column –	If the characteristic or behavior has been mastered and occurs consistently as a part of the child's behavior.

The *Humanics National Child Assessment Form* is designed to help the teacher observe the child in different areas of development and to follow changes. It is not a normative instrument, which means it is not to be used to compare one child with another. It is to be used as a tool in planning educational and developmental experiences for the child, and is not designed for diagnostic or clinical evaluations. The form is intended to be used by teachers and parents to better understand and relate to the individual needs of the child.

© 1982

HUMANICS LIMITED   ●   Post Office Box 7447   ●   Atlanta, Georgia 30309

SOCIAL-EMOTIONAL

Social-Emotional: Self-awareness and transactions with others. This includes expressing and controlling feelings, social awareness, self-concept development, relationship to parents and others.

Social-Emotional	Date: 9/15-9/25 Occurs Occasionally	Date: 9/15-9/25 Occurs Consistently	Date: ___ Occurs Occasionally	Date: ___ Occurs Consistently	Date: ___ Occurs Occasionally	Date: ___ Occurs Consistently
1. Focuses On Face — Focuses attention on face of another person.		✓ 9/18				
2. Responds To Voice — Turns head in response to voice.		9/18				
3. Smiles Responsively — Returns smile after seeing another person smiling.		9/18				
4. Discriminates Wants — Pushes away something not wanted.		9/18				
5. Plays Independently (I) — Plays alone for short periods of time.		9/18				
6. Plays Peek-a-boo — Plays peek-a-boo or smiles when you appear in peek-a-boo games		9/20				
7. Presents Objects — Hands object such as a toy to another person.		9/20				
8. Plays Simple Game — Plays simple rhythm games such as pat a cake with others.						
9. Plays Catch — Plays "catch" with another person by rolling a ball back and forth.						
10. Makes Wants Known — Points or calls to get desired object.	9/20					

11. Shows Familiar Object	Offers or shows a toy to another child.				
12. Plays Independently (II)	Plays independently of other children, occasionally interacting with them.				
13. Talks To Other Children	Talks or babbles to other children while playing near them.				
14. Begins Removing Clothing	Removes at least one piece of clothing, such as a sock.				
15. Identifies Familiar Person	Refers to a familiar person by name.				
16. Knows Own Name	Says first name when asked for it.				
17. Interacts With Other Children	Chooses to join a group of 2-3 children for a short time.				
18. Expresses Feelings	Uses words to express feelings of happiness, sadness, and anger.				

COMMENTS AND NOTES:

9/25 Sara is able to respond to others in her environment. She wants her needs known. She is old enough is beginning to make a few attempts able to interact with other children.

LANGUAGE

Making speech sounds and developing communication skills. This involves progression from babbling to labeling to speaking in sentences.

Language		Date: 9/6-9/25 Occurs Occasionally	Date: 9/6-9/25 Occurs Consistently	Date: ___ Occurs Occasionally	Date: ___ Occurs Consistently	Date: ___ Occurs Occasionally	Date: ___ Occurs Consistently
19. Laughs	Laughs out loud.		✓ 9/16				
20. Utters Speech Sounds (I)	Makes two different speech sounds. (examples: ba, da, ca, etc.)		✓ 9/16				
21. Babbles Responsively	Babbles back in response to adult talking.		✓ 9/16				
22. Connects Sounds	Strings different sounds together without meaning.		✓ 9/16				
23. Repeats Same Sound	Says da-da-da or ma-ma-ma (or equivalent) without specific reference to parent(s).		✓ 9/20				
24. Utters Speech Sounds (II)	Makes four different speech sounds.		✓ 9/20				
25. Imitates Sounds	Imitates sounds others make.		✓ 9/20				
26. Refers to Parent(s)	Says dada or mama (or equivalent) in reference to parent(s).	9/20					
27. Responds to Instructions	Responds to simple instructions such as no, stop, come here.						
28. Identifies Picture	Points to appropriate picture when told "Show me the _____."						

29. Verbally Identifies Need	Uses words to make wants known.			
30. Speaks Words	Has ten definite words in vocabulary.			
31. Makes Own Sentences	Makes three-word sentences (NOT just repeating parents' words).			
32. Identifies Position	Can show the location of an object that is: under, behind, or in front of.			
33. Answers Question	Answers simple questions, who and what.			
34. Forms Plurals	Adds 's' to words to form plurals. (example: dogs, books)			
35. Identifies Action	Identifies action in pictures (example: "The dog is running.")			
36. Combines Thoughts	Can express two thoughts combined. (for example, "When mommy comes, I'm going home.")			

COMMENTS AND NOTES:

9/30 Lara is emerging from the babbling stage. Her primary sounds (primary words) are beginning to take on meaning, e.g. "mama."

COGNITIVE

Cognitive	Acquiring and using information. This involves processes such as exploring, manipulation, making associations and problem solving.	Date: 9/15-9/25		Date: _____		Date: _____	
		Occurs Occasionally	Occurs Consistently	Occurs Occasionally	Occurs Consistently	Occurs Occasionally	Occurs Consistently
37. Explores Objects	Carries object in hand to mouth.		✓ 9/16				
38. Connects Sight With Sound	Looks in the direction of a sound.		✓ 9/16				
39. Discriminates Need	Accepts only milk or food; rejects other objects if placed in mouth when hungry.		✓ 9/16				
40. Follows Falling Object	Looks for an object after seeing it fall.		✓ 9/16				
41. Sustains Activity	Pulls repeatedly a cord attached to overhead bells or mobile.		✓ 9/17				
42. Finds Partially Hidden Toy	Finds and exposes partially hidden toy.						
43. Retrieves Object	Pulls strings to obtain object attached to it.		✓ 9/17				
44. Locates Desired Object	Moves object aside in order to reach another desired object.		✓ 9/17				
45. Searches For Hidden Object (I)	When hidden object is moved from one place to another, child continues to search in first place.	✓ 9/17					
46. Reveals Hidden Object	Unwraps a covered package to discover its contents.	✓ 9/17					

47. Searches For Hidden Object (II)	When hidden object is moved from one place to another, child searches in the new place.		
48. Identifies Body Parts	Points to three parts of own body.		
49. Identifies Familiar Objects	Can identify requested item from selection of three familiar toys.		
50. Recognizes Shapes	Fits circle, square, and triangle shape into holes of the same shapes.		
51. Understands Quantity	Knows concept of quantity, one and more than one.		
52. Matches Objects	Can pick a matching object from a group of three objects when told "Show me one like this."		
53. Works Puzzle	Works a 3-4 piece puzzle.		
54. Discriminates Size	Discriminates size: big and small, long and short.		

COMMENTS AND NOTES:

Lara is responding to her environment. She is using her senses to explore the environment. Her hearing and sight are being used to find and respond to incidentals. She cannot use words yet to express her desires.

GROSS MOTOR

Gross Motor — Using arms, legs, and torso with control and efficiency. This consists of large muscle skills such as reaching, crawling, balancing, standing and walking.

Gross Motor		Date: 9/15-9/25 Occurs Occasionally	Occurs Consistently	Date: _____ Occurs Occasionally	Occurs Consistently	Date: _____ Occurs Occasionally	Occurs Consistently
55. Holds Head And Chest Up	Holds head and chest up lying on stomach.	✓ 9/15					
56. Rolls To Side	Rolls from back to side.	✓ 9/15					
57. Swipes	Swipes at hanging objects.	✓ 9/15					
58. Crawls	Crawls on stomach.	✓ 9/15					
59. Holds Bottle	Holds bottle while being fed.	✓ 9/15					
60. Turns Body	From sitting position, turns body in response to rattling toy.	✓ 9/15					
61. Crawls After Ball	Moves a ball and crawls after it.	✓ 9/15					
62. Pulls up	Pulls self to standing position.	✓ 9/15					
63. Walks With Support	Walks while hands are held or holding to furniture.	✓ 9/16					
64. Walks Without Support	Walks forward without support, may fall occasionally.	✓ 9/16					

65. Squats	Squats down and stands back up without support.	✓ 9/25		
66. Walks Backward	Walks backward.	✓ 9/25		
67. Carries Large Object	Carries a large object (such as a large ball) while walking.			
68. Kicks Ball	Kicks a ball with one foot.			
69. Jumps In Place	Jumps in place with both feet.			
70. Balances On One Foot	Stands on one foot at a time with help.			
71. Rides Tricycle	Rides a tricycle.			
72. Walks On Tiptoes	Walks five steps on tiptoes.			

COMMENTS AND NOTES:

Tara has developed to the stage of walking. She is beginning to squat and walks backward.

FINE MOTOR

Fine Motor   Using hands, fingers, and eyes with control and efficiency. This consists of small muscle skills such as grasping, manipulating, stacking, and scribbling.

		Date: 9/15-9/25		Date: ___		Date: ___	
		Occurs Occasionally	Occurs Consistently	Occurs Occasionally	Occurs Consistently	Occurs Occasionally	Occurs Consistently
73. Holds Rattle	Holds rattle placed in hand.		✓ 9/15				
74. Follows Moving Object (I)	Eyes and head follow side to side motion of an object. (Child lying on back.)		✓ 9/15				
75. Follows Moving Object (II)	Eyes and head follow an object moved from above eyes to behind head. (Child lying on back.)		✓ 9/15				
76. Feeds Self	Feeds self cracker or teething biscuit.		✓ 9/15				
77. Exchanges Object Between Hands	Passes object from one hand to another.		✓ 9/15				
78. Picks Up Block	Picks up a one-inch block.		✓ 9/15				
79. Brings Objects Together	Bangs two blocks together, one in each hand.		✓ 9/15				
80. Puts Objects Into Container	Puts small objects through a slot into a container.		✓ 9/15				
81. Grasps Tiny Object	Grasps raisin or other tiny object with thumb or forefinger.		✓ 9/16				
82. Fits Ring Onto Peg	Fits a 2"-4" ring onto a peg.	✓ 9/20					

83.	Drinks From Cup	Drinks from a cup or glass without help, may spill occasionally.	✓ 9/20						
84.	Brings Spoon To Food	Holds a spoon and dips into food.	✓ 9/25						
85.	Turns Pages	Turns pages of a book, maybe several at a time.	✓ 9/25						
86.	Stacks Blocks (I)	Stacks a tower of four one-inch blocks.							
87.	Scribbles	Stays on large paper while scribbling.							
88.	Strings Beads	Strings five one-inch beads.							
89.	Stacks Blocks (II)	Stacks a tower of eight one-inch blocks.							
90.	Unbuttons Buttons	Unbuttons large buttons.							

COMMENTS AND NOTES:

INDIVIDUALIZED EDUCATIONAL PROGRAM

Child's Name _____

Person Responsible for Implementing _____   Date _____

Complete the individualized educational program based on assessment, observational and other information about the child. Circle appropriate item numbers below to indicate APPEARED behavior, cross(x) numbers to indicate STABILIZED behavior.

What Child Can Do	Goals and Objectives	Monitoring Child's Progress: When and How
Social Emotional — From the Assessment: 1 2 3 4 5 6 7 8 9 10 11 12 13 14 15 16 17 18	Annual Goals: Instructional Objectives:	
Language — From the Assessment: 19 20 21 22 23 24 25 26 27 28 29 30 31 32 33 34 35 36	Annual Goals: Instructional Objectives:	
Cognitive — From the Assessment: 37 38 39 40 41 42 43 44 45 46 47 48 49 50 51 52 53 54	Annual Goals: Instructional Objectives:	
Motor Skills — From the Assessment: (gross) 55 56 57 58 59 60 61 62 63 64 65 66 67 68 69 70 71 72 (fine) 73 74 75 76 77 78 79 80 81 82 83 84 85 86 87 88 89 90	Annual Goals: Instructional Objectives:	

Educational Program

Time spent in educational activities (Home/Center) _____

Plan developed by _____

Beginning Date _____   Ending Date _____

Parents participated in Meeting   Yes   No

Parents concur with I.E.P.   Yes   No

Parent signature _____

Humanics Limited/P.O.Box 7447/Atlanta, GA. 30309

164

The Successful Teacher's Most Valuable Resource!

EDUCATION

THE EARLI PROGRAM
Excellent language development program! Volume I contains developmentally sequenced lessons in verbal receptive language; Volume II, expressive language. Use as a primary, supplemental or rehabilitative language program.

Volume I	HL-067-7	$14.95
Volume II	HL-074-X	$14.95

LEARNING ENVIRONMENTS FOR CHILDREN
A practical manual for creating efficient, pleasant and stress-free learning environments for children centers. Make the best possible use of your center's space!

HL-065-0 $12.95

COMPETENCIES:
A Self-Study Guide to Teaching Competencies in Early Childhood Education
This comprehensive guide is ideal for evaluating or improving your competency in early childhood education or preparing for the CDA credential.

HL-024-3 $12.95

LOOKING AT CHILDREN:
Field Experiences in Child Study
A series of fourteen units made up of structured exercises dealing with such issues as language development, play and moral development in children. A fresh new approach to learning materials for early childhood educators.

HL-001-4 $14.95

YOUNG CHILDREN'S BEHAVIOR:
Implementing Your Goals
A variety of up-to-date approaches to discipline and guidance to help you deal more effectively with children. Also an excellent addition to CDA and competency-based training programs.

HL-015-4 $8.95

NUTS AND BOLTS
The ultimate guide to classroom organization and management of an early learning environment. Provides complete guidelines for setting up an early learning center; also excellent for improving an existing school system.

HL-063-4 $8.95

READING ROOTS:
Teach Your Child
Teach your child a basic reading vocabulary centered around the colors of his crayons before he enters school. Enjoyable coloring and matching activities make learning to read fun for both you and your child.

HL-070-7 $10.95

BACK TO BASICS IN READING MADE FUN
Refreshing and innovative approach to teaching basic reading skills which will delight and stimulate students. Over 100 creative games and projects to use in designing exciting reading materials.

HL-060-X $14.95

ACTIVITY BOOKS

EARLY CHILDHOOD ACTIVITIES:
A Treasury of Ideas from Worldwide Sources
A virtual encyclopedia of projects, games and activities for children aged 3 to 7, containing over 500 different child-tested activities drawn from a variety of teaching systems. The ultimate activity book!

HL-066-9 $16.95

VANILLA MANILA FOLDER GAMES
Make exciting and stimulating Vanilla Manila Folder Games quickly and easily with simple manila file folders and colored marking pens. Unique learning activities designed for children aged 3 to 8.

HL-059-6 $14.95

HANDBOOK OF LEARNING ACTIVITIES
Over 125 exciting, enjoyable activities and projects for young children in the areas of math, health and safety, play, movement, science, social studies, art, language development, puppetry and more!

HL-058-8 $14.95

MONTH BY MONTH ACTIVITY GUIDE FOR THE PRIMARY GRADES
Month by Month gives you a succinct guide to the effective recruitment and utilization of teachers' aides plus a full year's worth of fun-filled educational activities in such areas as reading, math, art, and science.

HL-061-8 $14.95

ART PROJECTS FOR YOUNG CHILDREN
Build a basic art program of stimulating projects on a limited budget and time schedule with Art Projects. Contains over 100 fun-filled projects in the areas of drawing, painting, puppets, clay, printing and more!

HL-051-0 $14.95

AEROSPACE PROJECTS FOR YOUNG CHILDREN
Introduce children to the fascinating field of aerospace with the exciting and informative projects and field trip suggestions. Contributors include over 30 aviation/aerospace agencies and personnel.

HL-052-9 $12.95

CHILD'S PLAY:
An Activities and Materials Handbook
An eclectic selection of fun-filled activities for preschool children designed to lend excitement to the learning process. Activities include puppets, mobiles, poetry, songs and more.

HL-003-0 $14.95

ENERGY:
A Curriculum for 3, 4 and 5 Year Olds
Help preschool children become aware of what energy is, the sources of energy, the uses of energy and wise energy use with the fun-filled activities, songs and games included in this innovative manual.

HL-069-3 $9.95

Humanics Publications

PARENT INVOLVEMENT

LOVE NOTES

A one year's supply of ready-to-use "Love Notes" to send home with the child to the parent. A novel and charming way to help parents enrich their parenting skills.

HL-068-5   **$19.95**

WORKING PARENTS:

How To Be Happy With Your Children

Dozens of easy and effective techniques and activities which will promote a constructive and enjoyable home and family life for the child and the working parent.

HL-006-5   **$9.95**

WORKING TOGETHER:

A Guide To Parent Involvement

Ideal guide for those wishing to launch a new parent involvement program or improve existing parent/school communication and interaction. Favorably reviewed by the National Association for Education of Young Children.

HL-002-2   **$14.95**

PARENTS AND TEACHERS

An intelligent, effective and field-tested program for improving the working relationship between parents and teachers. Now being used successfully in educational settings across the country.

HL-050-2   **$12.95**

ASSESSMENT

CHILDREN'S ADAPTIVE BEHAVIOR SCALE (CABS)

CABS is the first of its kind—a direct assessment tool which achieves the most complete measurement of adaptive behavior available today. Designed for children aged 5 to 11; quick and easy to administer.

HL-054-5   **$19.95**

THE LOLLIPOP TEST

A Diagnostic Screening Test of School Readiness

Based on the latest research in school readiness, this culture-free test effectively measures children's readiness strengths and weaknesses. Included is all you need to give, score and interpret the test.

HL-028-6   **$19.95**

ORIENTATION TO PRESCHOOL ASSESSMENT

Combines vital child development concepts into one integrated system of child observation and assessment. This is also the user's guide to the Humanics National Child Assessment Form—Age 3 to 6.

HL-020-0   **$14.95**

ORIENTATION TO INFANT & TODDLER ASSESSMENT

User's guide to the Humanics National Child Assessment Form—Age 0 to 3. Integrates critical concepts of child development into one effective system of observation and assessment.

HL-064-2   **$14.95**

SOCIAL SERVICES

HUMANICS LIMITED SYSTEM FOR RECORD KEEPING

Designed to meet all record keeping needs of family oriented social service agencies, this guide integrates the child, family, social worker and community into one coherent network. Also the user's guide to proper use of Humanics Limited Record Keeping forms.

HL-027-8   **$12.95**

REAL TALK:

Exercises in Friendship and Helping Skills

Real Talk teaches students basic skills in interpersonal relationships through such methods as role-playing and modeling. An ideal human relations course for elementary, junior high and high schools.

| Teacher's Manual | HL-026-X | $ 7.95 |
| Student's Manual | HL-025-1 | $12.95 |

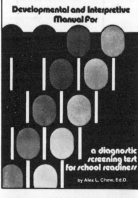

HUMANICS LIMITED

P.O. Box 7447
Atlanta, Georgia 30309
(404) 874-2176

ORDER FORM

HUMANICS LIMITED
P.O. BOX 7447/Atlanta, Georgia 30309

FOR FAST SERVICE
CALL COLLECT (404) 874-2176

QUANTITY ORDERED	ORDER NO.	BOOK TITLE	UNIT PRICE	TOTAL PRICE

☐ Payment Enclosed

☐ Institutional Purchase Order No. _____

☐ Bill my Credit Card

WHEN USING A CREDIT CARD, PLEASE CHECK PROPER BOX AND GIVE APPROPRIATE CARD AND NUMBER INFORMATION.

MASTER CARD ☐   VISA ☐

Credit Card No. [ ][ ][ ][ ][ ][ ][ ][ ][ ][ ][ ][ ][ ][ ][ ][ ]

Master Card Interbank No. [ ][ ][ ][ ][ ]   Exp. Date month/year [ ][ ][ ][ ][ ]

Authorized Signature (Order must be signed) _____

Subtotal _____

Georgia residents add 5% sales tax _____

Add shipping and handling charges _____

TOTAL ORDER _____

TO:

Ship to:
NAME _____
ADDRESS _____
CITY/STATE _____ ZIP _____
TELEPHONE _____ ( ) _____

Shipping and Handling Charges

Up to $10.00 add	$1.60
$10.01 to $20.00 add	$2.60
$20.01 to $40.00 add	$3.60
$40.01 to $70.00 add	$4.60
$70.01 to $100.00 add	$5.60
$100.01 to $125.00 add	$6.60
$125.01 to $150.00 add	$7.60
$150.01 to $175.00 add	$8.60
$175.01 to $200.00 add	$9.60

Orders over $200 vary depending on method of shipment.

Humanics National Child Assessment Form

Birth to Three

Marsha Kaufman, Ph.D. and T. Thomas McMurrain, Ph.D.

ABOUT THE FORM

The *Humanics National Child Assessment Form* is a checklist of skills and behaviors a child is likely to develop from birth to three years of age. Each item in the checklist is a sample of many related skills and behaviors and in that sense serves as an index of more general characteristics of development. Items in the Assessment Form are grouped into five scales that represent areas of child development: **Social-Emotional, Language, Cognitive, Gross Motor** and **Fine Motor.**

Within each scale, the items are arranged in a developmental sequence, and space is provided for assessing the child three times during the year. The Child Development Profile allows a visual representation of the child's ratings on each scale at the time of each assessment.

A NOTE TO THE PARENT

No one knows more about the development of your child than you do. This checklist is to structure some topics you and the teacher will discuss about your child. You may often want to add your own opinions and observations about your child's development. The information you and the teacher share is very important in designing an educational experience which will respond to and stimulate the individual nature and personality of your child.

DIRECTIONS

Complete all the items in the Assessment Form by observing the child in everyday play activities, or, if necessary, structuring special situations to let you observe the described behavior.

Mark each item as follows:

Make No Check Mark —

If the characteristic is not present or the behavior does not occur.

Check in the "Occurs Occasionally" Column —

If the characteristic or behavior is sometimes present, but it is not a consistent part of the behavior. The behavior has occurred occasionally but is not firmly mastered or developed.

Check in the "Occurs Consistently" Column —

If the characteristic or behavior has been mastered and occurs consistently as a part of the child's behavior.

The *Humanics National Child Assessment Form* is designed to help the teacher observe the child in different areas of development and to follow changes. It is not a normative instrument, which means it is not to be used to compare one child with another. It is to be used as a tool in planning educational and developmental experiences for the child, and is not designed for diagnostic or clinical evaluation. The form is intended to be used by teachers and parents to better understand and relate to the individual needs of the child.

© 1982

HUMANICS LIMITED • Post Office Box 7447 • Atlanta, Georgia 30309

Child's Name

Age   Date of Birth

Child Development Class

Teacher

Teacher Aide

Child Development Center

SOCIAL-EMOTIONAL

Self-awareness and transactions with others. This includes expressing and controlling feelings, social awareness, self-concept development, relationship to parents and others.

Social-Emotional	Date: ___ Occurs Occasionally	Occurs Consistently	Date: ___ Occurs Occasionally	Occurs Consistently	Date: ___ Occurs Occasionally	Occurs Consistently
1. Focuses On Face — Focuses attention on face of another person.						
2. Responds To Voice — Turns head in response to voice.						
3. Smiles Responsively — Returns smile after seeing another person smiling.						
4. Discriminates Wants — Pushes away something not wanted.						
5. Plays Independently (I) — Plays alone for short periods of time.						
6. Plays Peek-a-boo — Plays peek-a-boo or smiles when you appear in peek-a-boo games						
7. Presents Objects — Hands object such as a toy to another person.						
8. Plays Simple Game — Plays simple rhythm games such as pat a cake with others.						
9. Plays Catch — Plays "catch" with another person by rolling a ball back and forth.						
10. Makes Wants Known — Points or calls to get desired object.						

11.	Shows Familiar Object	Offers or shows a toy to another child.	
12.	Plays Independently (II)	Plays independently of other children, occasionally interacting with them.	
13.	Talks To Other Children	Talks or babbles to other children while playing near them.	
14.	Begins Removing Clothing	Removes at least one piece of clothing, such as a sock.	
15.	Identifies Familiar Person	Refers to a familiar person by name.	
16.	Knows Own Name	Says first name when asked for it.	
17.	Interacts With Other Children	Chooses to join a group of 2-3 children for a short time.	
18.	Expresses Feelings	Uses words to express feelings of happiness, sadness, and anger.	

COMMENTS AND NOTES:

LANGUAGE

Making speech sounds and developing communication skills. This involves progression from babbling to labeling to speaking in sentences.

Language		Date: _____		Date: _____		Date: _____	
		Occurs Occasionally	Occurs Consistently	Occurs Occasionally	Occurs Consistently	Occurs Occasionally	Occurs Consistently
19. Laughs	Laughs out loud.						
20. Utters Speech Sounds (I)	Makes two different speech sounds. (examples: ba, da, ca, etc.)						
21. Babbles Responsively	Babbles back in response to adult talking.						
22. Connects Sounds	Strings different sounds together without meaning.						
23. Repeats Same Sound	Says da-da-da or ma-ma-ma (or equivalent) without specific reference to parent(s).						
24. Utters Speech Sounds (II)	Makes four different speech sounds.						
25. Imitates Sounds	Imitates sounds others make.						
26. Refers to Parent(s)	Says dada or mama (or equivalent) in reference to parent(s).						
27. Responds to Instructions	Responds to simple instructions such as no, stop, come here.						
28. Identifies Picture	Points to appropriate picture when told "Show me the _____."						

29.	Verbally Identifies Need	Uses words to make wants known.			
30.	Speaks Words	Has ten definite words in vocabulary.			
31.	Makes Own Sentences	Makes three-word sentences (NOT just repeating parents' words).			
32.	Identifies Position	Can show the location of an object that is: under, behind, or in front of.			
33.	Answers Question	Answers simple questions, who and what.			
34.	Forms Plurals	Adds 's' to words to form plurals. (example: dogs, books)			
35.	Identifies Action	Identifies action in pictures (example: "The dog is running.")			
36.	Combines Thoughts	Can express two thoughts combined. (for example, "When mommy comes, I'm going home.")			

COMMENTS AND NOTES:

COGNITIVE

Cognitive — Acquiring and using information. This involves processes such as exploring, manipulation, making associations and problem solving.

	Date: ___		Date: ___		Date: ___	
	Occurs Occasionally	Occurs Consistently	Occurs Occasionally	Occurs Consistently	Occurs Occasionally	Occurs Consistently
37. Explores Objects — Carries object in hand to mouth.						
38. Connects Sight With Sound — Looks in the direction of a sound.						
39. Discriminates Need — Accepts only milk or food; rejects other objects if placed in mouth when hungry.						
40. Follows Falling Object — Looks for an object after seeing it fall.						
41. Sustains Activity — Pulls repeatedly a cord attached to overhead bells or mobile.						
42. Finds Partially Hidden Toy — Finds and exposes partially hidden toy.						
43. Retrieves Object — Pulls strings to obtain object attached to it.						
44. Locates Desired Object — Moves object aside in order to reach another desired object.						
45. Searches For Hidden Object (I) — When hidden object is moved from one place to another, child continues to search in first place.						
46. Reveals Hidden Object — Unwraps a covered package to discover its contents.						

47. Searches For Hidden Object (II)	When hidden object is moved from one place to another, child searches in the new place.					
48. Identifies Body Parts	Points to three parts of own body.					
49. Identifies Familiar Objects	Can identify requested item from selection of three familiar toys.					
50. Recognizes Shapes	Fits circle, square, and triangle shape into holes of the same shapes.					
51. Understands Quantity	Knows concept of quantity, one and more than one.					
52. Matches Objects	Can pick a matching object from a group of three objects when told "Show me one like this."					
53. Works Puzzle	Works a 3-4 piece puzzle.					
54. Discriminates Size	Discriminates size: big and small, long and short.					

COMMENTS AND NOTES:

GROSS MOTOR

Gross Motor	Using arms, legs, and torso with control and efficiency. This consists of large muscle skills such as reaching, crawling, balancing, standing and walking.	Date: ___ Occurs Occasionally	Occurs Consistently	Date: ___ Occurs Occasionally	Occurs Consistently	Date: ___ Occurs Occasionally	Occurs Consistently
55. Holds Head And Chest Up	Holds head and chest up lying on stomach.						
56. Rolls To Side	Rolls from back to side.						
57. Swipes	Swipes at hanging objects.						
58. Crawls	Crawls on stomach.						
59. Holds Bottle	Holds bottle while being fed.						
60. Turns Body	From sitting position, turns body in response to rattling toy.						
61. Crawls After Ball	Moves a ball and crawls after it.						
62. Pulls up	Pulls self to standing position.						
63. Walks With Support	Walks while hands are held or holding to furniture.						
64. Walks Without Support	Walks forward without support, may fall occasionally.						

65.	Squats	Squats down and stands back up without support.		
66.	Walks Backward	Walks backward.		
67.	Carries Large Object	Carries a large object (such as a large ball) while walking.		
68.	Kicks Ball	Kicks a ball with one foot.		
69.	Jumps In Place	Jumps in place with both feet.		
70.	Balances On One Foot	Stands on one foot at a time with help.		
71.	Rides Tricycle	Rides a tricycle.		
72.	Walks On Tiptoes	Walks five steps on tiptoes.		

COMMENTS AND NOTES:

FINE MOTOR

Fine Motor   Using hands, fingers, and eyes with control and efficiency. This consists of small muscle skills such as grasping, manipulating, stacking, and scribbling.

		Date: ____		Date: ____		Date: ____	
		Occurs Occasionally	Occurs Consistently	Occurs Occasionally	Occurs Consistently	Occurs Occasionally	Occurs Consistently
73. Holds Rattle	Holds rattle placed in hand.						
74. Follows Moving Object (I)	Eyes and head follow side to side motion of an object. (Child lying on back.)						
75. Follows Moving Object (II)	Eyes and head follow an object moved from above eyes to behind head. (Child lying on back.)						
76. Feeds Self	Feeds self cracker or teething biscuit.						
77. Exchanges Object Between Hands	Passes object from one hand to another.						
78. Picks Up Block	Picks up a one-inch block.						
79. Brings Objects Together	Bangs two blocks together, one in each hand.						
80. Puts Objects Into Container	Puts small objects through a slot into a container.						
81. Grasps Tiny Object	Grasps raisin or other tiny object with thumb or forefinger.						
82. Fits Ring Onto Peg	Fits a 2"-4" ring onto a peg.						

83.	Drinks From Cup	Drinks from a cup or glass without help, may spill occasionally.
84.	Brings Spoon To Food	Holds a spoon and dips into food.
85.	Turns Pages	Turns pages of a book, maybe several at a time.
86.	Stacks Blocks (I)	Stacks a tower of four one-inch blocks.
87.	Scribbles	Stays on large paper while scribbling.
88.	Strings Beads	Strings five one-inch beads.
89.	Stacks Blocks (II)	Stacks a tower of eight one-inch blocks.
90.	Unbuttons Buttons	Unbuttons large buttons.

COMMENTS AND NOTES:

CHILD DEVELOPMENT SUMMARY PROFILE

INSTRUCTIONS: Circle each item checked "occurs consistently" in each sub-scale (Social-Emotional, Language, Cognitive, Gross Motor, and Fine Motor) using one color, Circle each item checked "occurs occasionally" in each sub-scale in another color on the chart below.

1st ASSESSMENT   Date _____   Teacher _____

SOCIAL-EMOTIONAL	1	2	3	4	5	6	7	8	9	10	11	12	13	14	15	16	17	18
LANGUAGE	19	20	21	22	23	24	25	26	27	28	29	30	31	32	33	34	35	36
COGNITIVE	37	38	39	40	41	42	43	44	45	46	47	48	49	50	51	52	53	54
GROSS MOTOR	55	56	57	58	59	60	61	62	63	64	65	66	67	68	69	70	71	72
FINE MOTOR	73	74	75	76	77	78	79	80	81	82	83	84	85	86	87	88	89	90

2nd ASSESSMENT   Date _____   Teacher _____

SOCIAL-EMOTIONAL	1	2	3	4	5	6	7	8	9	10	11	12	13	14	15	16	17	18
LANGUAGE	19	20	21	22	23	24	25	26	27	28	29	30	31	32	33	34	35	36
COGNITIVE	37	38	39	40	41	42	43	44	45	46	47	48	49	50	51	52	53	54
GROSS MOTOR	55	56	57	58	59	60	61	62	63	64	65	66	67	68	69	70	71	72
FINE MOTOR	73	74	75	76	77	78	79	80	81	82	83	84	85	86	87	88	89	90

3rd ASSESSMENT   Date _____   Teacher _____

SOCIAL-EMOTIONAL	1	2	3	4	5	6	7	8	9	10	11	12	13	14	15	16	17	18
LANGUAGE	19	20	21	22	23	24	25	26	27	28	29	30	31	32	33	34	35	36
COGNITIVE	37	38	39	40	41	42	43	44	45	46	47	48	49	50	51	52	53	54
GROSS MOTOR	55	56	57	58	59	60	61	62	63	64	65	66	67	68	69	70	71	72
FINE MOTOR	73	74	75	76	77	78	79	80	81	82	83	84	85	86	87	88	89	90

HUMANICS LIMITED • 1182 West Peachtree Street • P.O. Box 7447 • Atlanta, Georgia 30307 • (404) 874-2176